Peace and Power

Building Communities
for the Future

Peace and Power

Building Communities for the Future

Fourth Edition
Peggy L. Chinn

JONES AND BARTLETT PUBLISHERS
Sudbury, Massachusetts
BOSTON   TORONTO   LONDON   SINGAPORE

World Headquarters

Jones and Bartlett Publishers
40 Tall Pine Drive
Sudbury, MA 01776
978-443-5000
info@jbpub.com
www.jbpub.com

Jones and Bartlett Publishers Canada
P.O. Box 19020
Toronto, ON M5S 1X1
CANADA

Jones and Bartlett Publishers International
Barb House, Barb Mews
London W6 7PA
UK

Printed in the United States of America
02 01 00 99 98   10 9 8 7 6 5 4 3 2 1

Dedicated in loving memory to

Charlene Eldridge Wheeler
August 26, 1944–March 30, 1993

Primary author of the first three editions of this book.

Her vision, wisdom, and persistent hard work were central to the conception and to the concrete reality of this book. Her spirit still lives within these pages, and within the hearts and minds of all of the women who worked with her in groups.

Contents

Acknowledgments

This book grew out of a desire shared by Charlene and myself to document in writing the women's wisdom that was passed on to us in the oral tradition and through lived example. For over a decade, we worked and played in groups of women dedicated to transformation. Out of our experiences emerged the ideas written in these pages. Many friends and colleagues shared our journey, and in a real sense share the story of this process.

Wilma Scott Heide, a dear friend and courageous women's movement leader of the early 1970s, gave Charlene and myself the inspiration and determination to venture into publishing the first edition of *Peace and Power* as Margaretdaughters, Inc.[1] She told us that when she first read the book, she wept, both from the joy of seeing feminist ideas presented in this way, and from the anguish of not having had the benefit of some of these insights in her early years of activist work. As we conveyed to her many times before her death in 1984, it is because of her own courageous living, and that of women like her, that we have been able to do the work on which these ideas are built.

Patricia Moccia, a woman of vision in our own generation, believed in the possibilities of this process for a wider circle, and initiated and facilitated the publication of the second edition by the National League for Nursing. She and Allan Graubard, Director of NLN Press, have encouraged and supported the continued publication of this book and the many changes that I have made in this edition.

The groups in which we worked together, and some in which I have worked since Charlene's death, have had a fundamental influence in shaping this book. Through these groups, we were given opportunities to live our values, and explore new ways of putting our values into action. These groups challenged our ideas and inspired new ideas and imagination of what kind of future we seek. I now name these groups, and individuals in them who have inspired, assisted, challenged, and modeled what now appear as ideas in this book.

The Emma Collective was a group of women who owned a women's bookstore in Buffalo, New York. Lisa Albrecht, a member of the Emma Collective at the time that we joined, was a marvelous guide and teacher as Charlene and I first began to develop the insights that made this book possible. The Emma Collective women were dedicated to a verbal tradition that put language to the process, modeling ways to truly do what we know and know what we do. The name *Emma* was chosen to honor literary and historical women named Emma, who are models of women's strength and wisdom.

The Women's Studies Program at the State University of New York at Buffalo has a tradition since the late 1960s of using a rotating chair process in their meetings and class gatherings. We first learned about transformation in classrooms and institutions by being part of some of their gatherings.

Various coalitions of women in the Buffalo community, including the Voices of Women Writers Coalition (1982) and International Women's Day (IWD) Coalitions (1982–86), provided "classrooms" in which we learned the realities of women's community activism. In 1983, the IWD Coalition invited Wilma Scott Heide to speak, making possible the important connection Charlene and I formed with Wilma.

Cassandra: Radical Feminist Nurses Network (1982–1989) was a national network of nurses committed to developing feminist analyses of issues in nursing and women's health. Our gatherings, as well as our struggles to work together across long distances to carry out responsibilities for the *News Journal* and the *Webstership* list, contributed immeasurably to shaping our ideals of community.

The Friendship Collective (1987–1989) was a group of nurses who gathered to study the meaning and significance of women's friendships in nursing. Members of this group were: Elizabeth Berrey, Peggy Chinn, Cathy Kane, Christine Madsen, Adrienne Roy, Charlene Eldridge Wheeler, and Elizabeth Mathier Wheeler. Throughout this book are many examples from the experiences of this group largely because of Elizabeth Berrey's leadership, sustained a deep commitment to living peace and power through our time together.

Participants in the Feminism and Nursing class at the State University of New York at Buffalo, Spring, 1982 were particularly influential in our early determination to see these ideas in print. Anne Montes, Adrienne Roy and Penny DeRaps, whom Charlene and I first met in that class, remained close friends and provided many forms of love and support that made this work possible.

The Faculty of Nursing at the University of Technology, Sydney, Kuring-Gai Campus in New South Wales, Australia, participated in a workshop (December 1990) that Charlene and I conducted which provided us with new insights about the use of the Process in traditional institutions. The department Chair, Judy Lumby, made this workshop possible. In a loving and respectful way, she explored with us some of the most difficult aspects of shifting values in a context where hierarchical ideals reign supreme.

During a 1990 visit to Deakin University in Geelong, Victoria, Australia, we were also able to explore more fully the philosophic ideas that informed the approaches we describe here. Pat Hickson and Cheryle Moss shared many discussions about the intersections between feminist values and traditional philosophy.

In the time between the publication of the 2nd and 3rd editions, Charlene and I relocated geographically to Denver, Colorado. We prepared the third edition while working with groups of students in the graduate programs of the School of Nursing, many of whom began to use peace and power processes in various ways in their own work. Carole Schroeder and her children Ben and Morgan, supported us through the challenges of revising a book about peace while our country was again waging war. Fran Reeder and Jean Watson, faculty in the School of Nursing, have used peace and power processes in their classes over the past several years, bringing new dimensions of possibilities to creating transformations in institutions.

When Charlene was facing her last days in the ravages of systemic lupus, we both lived a remarkable form of peace and power in the loving company of women who cared for us and created a community to hold the experience of dying. Chris Tanner and Jan Kemp built the bridge between the rule-driven hierarchical hospital establishment, and our visions of community, to make it possible for us to be with Charlene throughout her last days. Unable to speak, Charlene used a notepad to communicate, engaging the physicians and nurses in our community. She called for circling among us to hear each of our perspectives as to what she should choose when faced with medical decisions. When she could no longer communicate, we sang her name, stayed with her day and night, lovingly nursing her through a transition none of us wanted to choose.

Since Charlene's death, I have experienced many challenges that have stretched the limits of my capacity to envision a transformed and transformative community. I now acknowledge women who have traveled the rough paths with me over the past two years, and who have provided support and inspiration to move into a new future. Sue Hagedorn, who has been a dear friend and colleague, used peace and power processes in her work with teen-age women exploring the experience of menarche. While I was not part of the group she worked with, I learned many new possibilities as I listened to Sue's stories from this remarkable experience.[2] Kathy Maeve, who demonstrates amazing talents of challenging the status quo with love and compassion, facilitated a discussion group during the fall of 1994 in which a group of us experienced community for a brief time in the face of deep institutional turmoil. Janet Kemp, who nursed Charlene almost daily for the last four months of her life, has remained a dear friend, connecting with my community of friends from all over the world. Judith Claire in Adelaide, South Australia, provided a loving and healing space, and affirmation of what can evolve in groups when there is an intention of peace.

Acknowledgments

There are many individuals in groups with whom I now work who provide me places to try new ideas and practice the skills of *Peace and Power*. I teach the process to groups in the community, learning from them ways to adapt and develop skills of *Peace and Power*. I am particularly indebted to Julia Carpenter and Natural Healing Expressions for their recent commitment to working with the process in their healing work.

Since the publication of the third edition, titled *Peace and Power: A Handbook of Feminist Process*, the book has received steadily growing interest from groups all over the world. It has been used by many in the midst of enormous adversity.[3] According to mediator, Merle Lefkoff, "The women of the Center for Women War Victims in Zagreb, Croatia, are using *Peace and Power* processes for organizational development in their work in refugee camps, where they are setting up and facilitating women's support groups." Many women there are suffering the effects of genocidal rape, enforced pregnancies resulting in the devastation of family bloodlines, torture, mutilation, and murder as consequences of war. The Center uses *Peace and Power* to guide groups in reaching consensus and to strengthen the connection between group cohesiveness and community empowerment.

Peace and Power has been translated into Portuguese, German, Spanish, Serbo-Croatian and Macedonian-Albanian. I am aware of the ideas being integrated into women's work in Japan, Australia, New Zealand, and Taiwan and my work with increasingly diverse groups convinces me that it is time to bring the ideas rooted in women's experience to a broad circle of participants—many of whom are turning to women's wisdom to heal, to nurture, to find peace and harmony. The change in the title to *Peace and Power: Building Communities for the Future,* acknowledges that the time has come to build bridges, to seek understanding, to create loving, respectful and nurturing communities with all who will join this journey. And so, in tribute to my experiences of doing just that with Charlene, and in recognition of possibilities for the future we could not have imagined 15 years ago, I give to you, the reader, this fourth edition of *Peace and Power*.

Prologue

Community. A word of many connotations—a word overused until its meanings are so diffuse as to be almost useless. Yet the images it evokes, the deep longings and memories it can stir, represent something that human beings have created and recreated since time immemorial, out of our profound need for connection among ourselves and with Mother Earth.

Helen Forsey, 1993[1]

We are tired to death of swimming upstream alone; we want to feel grounded, connected, to be able to touch the earth and put down roots. We are searching for simplicity and balance in our lives, for comradeship and challenge in our work and our relationships. We feel a need for hope, for possibilities in the midst of despair, for integrity and wholeness in the struggle against alienation, for stability in place of rootlessness, for nurturing and closeness based on equality and respect, not on obligation and exploitation. These needs dictate the journey that leads us to community.

Helen Forsey, 1993[2]

. . . community building must be a feminist project, and particularly an ecofeminist one. An understanding of how and why women have been subjugated by patriarchy is absolutely fundamental to any rebuilding of

human society, or we will delude ourselves and our revolutions will bring us right back to the same behavior with which we started.

Judith Plant, 1993[3]

If you have grown dissatisfied with the way things work in groups you belong to, and find yourself thinking "there has got to be a better way," you are not alone. Many people are seeking alternative ways to build meaningful relationships and effective ways of working together in all sorts of communities and groups. This book gives you a "value map" to think about alternatives, specific guidelines for working with others to create meaningful community, and examples of real groups that serve as models of *Peace and Power* processes.

Peace and Power processes are specific actions that arise from carefully chosen values. In turn, the actions make the chosen values real—the values become visible and felt because they are acted upon. These processes are feminist because they create *practices* that are specifically designed to overcome the disadvantages of, or oppressions that have affected women in particular. The practices are informed by consciousness of that which is embedded in patriarchal and oppressive contexts, *and* by consciousness of practices that can often be found in places where women conduct their own affairs.[4] While the practices were developed from the experience of women, as is typical of feminist approaches in other arenas (for example, teaching or doing research), the processes of *Peace and Power* are specifically designed to overcome all oppressions and practices that arise from imbalances of power.

Women have traditionally been peacemakers, but women's peace-making work, and the skills it requires, have been privatized and invisible.[5] In part because this work has been invisible, exactly what skills are required to be effective are not known or practiced in the public world. The values that are often found in places where women conduct their own affairs can be described; the skills and actions and abilities that go with those values are what constitute the *Peace and Power* processes described in this book. The close link between values and action is called "doing what we know, and knowing what we do."

Women in the feminist tradition have been and are continuing to re-member[6] the wisdom of Doing what we Know, and of Knowing what we Do. While we may not always manage to Do what we Know, the wisdom survives and is being re-learned with every attempt, with every re-attempt. The Knowing is so deeply buried, under layers and layers of patriarchal learning and conditioning, that the Trying feels extremely tedious. It is at the same time exciting, affirming and encouraging. It becomes easier with every lived experience, especially within the context of a community that is loving and protective. Living and working in such a community is an experience that nurtures, that is healing of the mind, body and spirit. Indeed, *Peace and Power* values and practices are closely related to the tradition of women as healers.[7]

Like much of women's wisdom, *Peace and Power* processes have been preserved primarily in oral traditions. The written word provides a form that can be more or less enduring in a concrete way, but at the same time becomes static, and vulnerable to destruction. For centuries, women scholars have recorded women's wisdom into written form, but much of that writing has not survived.[8]

The spoken word, while seeming to disappear once the words are spoken, endures within the hearts and minds of listeners and speakers. Once spoken, it cannot be destroyed unless every person who has heard those words is destroyed. Speaking can also be an interaction, as the speaker and the listener attend to the responses of one another. The act of speaking is an emergence, a creation and a form that gives rise to new acts, new thoughts and new forms even as the speech occurs. The act of listening—hearing another's words gain expression—facilitates a co-creation and allows a fine-tuning of ideas that combines each person's perceptions as words are shared.

Speaking and language are crucial to co-creating processes of *Peace and Power*. For the most part, language uses patriarchal words. In the attempt to reflect values and practices that are often found in the company of women, new meanings and new words are created. When a listener does not comprehend the meanings, both actions and speaking are needed to make the new meanings clear. Fortunately, it is possible to convey the new meanings because in a sense, they are not new at all. They are part of everyone's experience, but have not had a language for expression. An example is the experience of peaceful, even energizing disagreement. There is no word for this in American English, but the experience is known to most people.

In this book you will find both old words with new meanings, and new words created to more fully express meanings associated with the *Peace and Power* processes. As a reader, you will not be able to observe actions that might enrich your comprehension. The stories that are included throughout the book will help to fill this void. Also, the book provides guidelines for thinking about, and for practicing, the new skills that are part of *Peace and Power* processes. You will, as you begin to create processes in your own time and space, begin to comprehend and create meanings that emerge from your own wisdom and experience.

By now you may have noticed that I refer to you, the reader, creating your own *Peace and Power* processes. While this book gives guidelines, suggestions, and practices that have been tried successfully in many situations, what this book presents is not the only way. There are many practices "out there" that groups create to suit their own purposes that are not described here. You will probably begin by using the practices described in this book, and gradually find your own path to create practices that are consistent with your chosen values, and with your circumstances.

It is important to take some time to consider if *Peace and Power* processes are "right" for you and your group. There are several questions you can ponder to help you and your group decide:[9]

> **Do we have a unity of purpose?** It is common for members of a group to have differing ideas about the group's purpose, but if you can identify a simple statement that reflects a common understanding of what you are all about, this unity is a good foundation for the work of *Peace and Power*.
>
> **Do we agree in principle that we seek to equalize the balance of power among everyone in the group?** If people in the group can answer "yes" to this question, *Peace and Power* processes are for you—the processes are designed to do just this.
>
> **How independent are we of external hierarchical structures?** The more your group is influenced by a hierarchical structure (for

example a college, corporation, or business), the more difficult it will be to enact *Peace and Power* processes. This will not be impossible, but realize that you may have to make major adjustments. Chapter 11 helps to address some of the challenges you will face. If you are relatively independent of an external hierarchical structure (for example, a community activist group, spiritual community, or intentional community), you will still be influenced by everyone's habits in hierarchical ways of being. But you will be relatively free to create your own processes consistent with *Peace and Power*, and to challenge the traditions of hierarchy that individuals bring into the group.

Are we all committed to having time together? It is not possible to develop cohesiveness and unity in a community unless you spend time together. You may not be able to be together often, but you need to have some regular and agreed-on time to be together. Not everyone has to be present each time your group meets, but everyone needs to know when and where the group meets. Everyone also needs to make a commitment to be there as regularly as possible.

Are members of the group willing to attend to the group's process? *Peace and Power* processes require taking time and turning attention to reflection on, and discussion of, the group's process. If you move to these processes, you will be doing much more than just taking care of business. *Peace and Power* assumes that the group is striving to bring values and actions into accord with one another. This is only possible if you take the time to discuss what is happening in the process, and together look carefully to see if indeed your values and your actions match.

Do we seek foundational change in ourselves and in the world at large? *Peace and Power* processes are designed to create change away from practices that oppress and alienate, toward practices that nurture and empower. These words may seem appealing and easy to embrace in principle. However, chances are that you and members of your group have learned how to interact in ways that alienate and divide, in ways that sustain privilege for some and disadvantage for others. Making a change to act and interact in cooperative and collective ways that build community challenges many practices that are habitual, and this requires new learning. If you use this process, be aware that you, along with everyone in your group, will be called upon to make changes.

If you think this book and this process are for you, here is a general description of what you will find:

The first two chapters provide the ideas, the values, and the assumptions upon which *Peace and Power* processes are built. Chapter 3 describes what it means to make the commitment to *Peace and Power* values and processes. Chapter 4 gives guidelines for forming a group's Principles of Unity. Chapters 5 through 8 provide descriptions of each component of the Process in action, focusing on what happens when your group gathers together. Chapter 9 provides guidelines for transforming conflict, including suggestions for individuals as well as for the group as a whole. Chapter 10 gives brief guidelines for periodic transitions, such as changes in group membership. Chapter 11 explores using *Peace and Power* processes within existing patriarchal systems, particularly in classrooms, committees, and other types of work groups.

The Notes at the end of the book, arranged by chapter, provide the traditional "references" to literature and to the women and groups of women who have helped to shape the ideas of *Peace and Power*. These notes also provide anecdotal commentary about the text itself, parenthetical ideas related to the text, experiences that inform the text, and literature that provides additional in-depth information about topics in the text. Like the traditions that have emerged in the work of other feminist authors, the notes are a valuable resource of information and quite readable in their own right.

Throughout, you will find examples that draw on personal experiences with *Peace and Power* processes. All examples are stories developed from real experiences. Some are composites of different experiences, designed to illustrate critical insights.

When Charlene and I wrote the third edition of this book, the United States had entered into another war—the Persian Gulf war. When the war "ended," peace did not exist. This was yet another grim reminder that peace is not merely the absence of war, and that re-definition of power is desperately needed. During that time, Charlene and I talked with many women who were also eager to explore how to create peace on earth, by beginning within, where we live and work, everyday, in ways that build on the values of *Peace and Power*.[10] We put many of the ideas together in the following list—a list that also forms images of communities for the future.

A Dozen and One Important Things You Can Do To Create Peace On Earth

1. Plant and nurture something that grows.

2. Practice the fine art of yielding—in your car, in conversation, etc.

3. Become active in a group that works on principles of cooperation, on principles of *Peace and Power*.

4. Fill your home, work, and commuting environments with visual and auditory images of peace and tranquility.

5. Do at least one thing to simplify your life *and* reduce your consumption of disposable products.

6. Do at least one thing to reduce your consumption of natural resources.

7. Move toward a vegetarian diet.

8. Learn and practice some form of meditation.

9. Learn and practice ways to reduce hostile interactions with others.

10. Exchange gentle forms of touch regularly.

11. Express appreciation to at least one individual or group every day.

12. Help three children learn three things on this list.

13. Pass this list along to someone else.

1

What It's All About: PEACE

If I believe so much must change, I must be willing to change myself.

Francis Moore Lappé, 1990[1]

Copper Woman warned Hai Nai Yu that the world would change and times might come when Knowing would not be the same as Doing. And she told her that Trying would always be very important.

Anne Cameron[2]

A few women, old now, and no longer strong. A few elder women who kept alive what the invader tried to destroy. Grandmothers and aunts. Mothers and sisters. Who must be honoured and cherished and protected even at risk of your own life. Who must be respected. At all times respected. Women who know that which we must try to learn again. Women who provide a nucleus on which we must build again. Women who will share with us if we ask them. Women who love us. And seeing candidates, who have been tested and found worthy, and who are learning the old wisdom. Young women who do not always manage to Do what they Know, and so need our love and help.

Anne Cameron[3]

. . . reflection and action, imagining and doing, are closely connected. We cannot act what we have not in some way thought.

Elise Boulding, 1988[4]

Peace is both intent and process. The kind of *Peace* that this book is about requires conscious awareness of what happens in a group. *Peace* requires that you Know what you do as an individual when you interact with others. *Peace* requires that you do what in your heart you know—that your chosen values guide your actions. *Peace* is the means and the end, the process and the product.

The ways of *Peace* are rooted in women's ancient wisdom. Much of that wisdom has been lost or obscured, but it can be found and reclaimed. In the face of modern stress, violence and destruction, people are turning to women's wisdom because it is about peace, creativity, love, respect, nurturing, growth, healing.[5]

The acronym that follows defines the idea of *Peace* as intent/ process. Each letter of the word PEACE represents a commitment that guides the ways in which individuals can choose to relate to one another within the context of group process.

Praxis

Empowerment

Awareness

Consensus

Evolvement

PRAXIS

Praxis is thoughtful reflection and action that occur in synchrony, in the direction of transforming the world.[6] Most people have limited knowledge of praxis, since we live in a time when "knowing" and "doing" are rarely the same. In western cultures, the message "Do as I say, not as I do" is a familiar one. When you choose to convey the message that: "I Know what I do, and I Do what I

Know," you begin to live your values. Praxis is *values made visible through deliberate action*. Your actions, chosen to reflect values of *Peace and Power*, become an ongoing cycle of constant renewal. As your actions are informed by your awareness of values, your thinking and your ideas are shaped and changed by your experiences with those actions.

EMPOWERMENT

Empowerment is growth of personal strength, power, and ability to enact one's own will and love for self in the context of love and respect for others. Empowerment is not self-indulgence, but rather is a form of strength that comes from real solidarity with and among those who seek PEACE.[7] Empowerment requires listening inwardly to your own senses as well as listening intently and actively to others, consciously taking in and forming strength.[8] Empowerment is not power-over other people, other creatures, or the earth. In fact, empowerment is only possible when individuals express respect and reverence for all other forms of life and ground the energy of the Self as one with the earth.

AWARENESS

Awareness is an active, growing knowledge of Self and others and the world in which you live. This means tuning into the moment. It also means a heightened, transcendent awareness that sees beyond the moment to the past and the future. The fundamental method of feminism is consciousness-raising, or seeing your world in a political and historical context. This is a vital transformation in a society that treats women's knowing and experience as abnormal or non-existent. With awareness comes a consciousness of "double-speak," where what is defined as "normal" is really abnormal; what is defined as "peace" is really war.[9]

CONSENSUS

Consensus is an active commitment to group solidarity and group integrity. It embodies cooperation and collectivity. While decision making by consensus is a part of *Peace and Power* processes, it is also an internal attitude which welcomes differences of opinion, and an openness to self-reflection.

A group's commitment to decision-making by consensus grows out of mutually defined Principles of Unity, where each individual's viewpoint is equally valued when group decisions are made. It means moving away from any action that exerts power over other individuals or groups. Rather, consensus grows from a full integration, a coming to terms with all perceptions that bear on a particular concern, issue, or decision.[10]

EVOLVEMENT

Evolvement is a commitment to growth, where change and transformation are conscious and deliberate. Evolvement can be likened to the cycles of the moon where new and old, life and death, and all phases are ultimately one. What remains constant is the cycle itself. As you experience group processes based on PEACE, you are changed. A group changes as circumstances shift, as individuals move in and out or become more or less involved, and as purposes or activities change. Growth and transformations are valued and celebrated with each new cycle.[11] You create your realities as you live them. There can be no mistakes, no disasters—only opportunities for re-creation.

PEACE IS NOT . . .

- letting things slide for the sake of friendship
- doing whatever is required to keep on good terms
- criticizing someone behind her back
- being silent at a meeting only to rant and rave afterwards
- letting things drift if they don't affect you personally

- playing safe in order to avoid confrontation
- manipulating someone to avoid open conflict
- coercing someone to do what you want
- hearing distortions of truth without refuting them
- indulging another's behavior when it is destructive
- withholding information in order to protect someone else

HAVING GOOD INTENTIONS IS NOT ENOUGH

Having the intent of *Peace* is critical when you enter a group interaction. However, intent is not enough. Actions that flow from intent are essential; actions are the critical test of intent. Examine how fully your actions flow with your intent by asking questions like these:

- Do I Know what I Do, and do I Do what I Know? (Praxis)
- Am I expressing my own will in the context of love and respect for others? (Empowerment)
- Am I fully aware of myself and others? (Awareness)
- Do I face conflicts openly and integrate differences in forming solutions? (Consensus)
- Do I value growth and change for myself, others and the group? (Evolvement)

2

How We Get There From Here: POWER

This transition in our concept of power is radical. It involves seeing power not as a property we own, not as something we exert over others, but as a verb, a process we participate in. This is a huge evolutionary shift.

Joanna Rogers Macy[1]

The challenge for us in developing our personal power is our willingness to recognize that power is within us and in our courageous choice to forgive and release anything that prevents this power from fully manifesting.

Diane Mariechild[2]

We must build a new model of power that is defined as presence: presence of awareness of my own strengths and weaknesses, a deep respect for the SELF of me and therefore a respect for the SELF of others. We must journey toward the individual wholeness of each within the group structure. We must soften and/or relax the barrier between the intellect and the emotions so that the powerful and wonderful material of the unconscious becomes available to the individual and the group. We must be present to self and to others. Power in and of itself is neutral. We must take responsibility for our own actions and choose to know our own intent and the intent of any group before we simply follow a plan of action.

Peace and Power

Power-over demands that we do things we don't choose to do. Power-of-presence means we choose carefully and understand our intentions.

Grace R. Rowan[3]

Power is the energy from which action arises. The kind of power that energizes PEACE is different from power as it is used in the world at large. Power, as it is used in the world at large, reflects a patriarchal ideal. Defined in patriarchal terms, power is the capacity to impose one's will on others, accompanied by a willingness to apply negative sanctions against those who oppose that will. This translates into a "love of power," where the fact of *having* the power becomes more important, more critical, than *what* that power is used for or what results from the use of that power. Any measure that is necessary to retain that power is considered justifiable. Further, individuals who are being manipulated or controlled do not recognize these underlying dynamics, because they are so thoroughly taught that the power structure, as it is set up, is the "only way." In this book this type of power is called "Power-Over."

The kind of power required to create and live PEACE reflects an ideal where the focus shifts to underlying values associated with the exercise of power, and what happens when power is used. What is valued is the capacity to be in harmony with others and with the earth, to join with others in directing your collective energies toward a future you seek together. In this book, this type of power is called "PEACE Power."[4]

In this chapter you will see these two types of powers contrasted. These are not the only types of powers that might be imagined. But they are both very important to consider if your group is moving toward creating a balance of power in your relations with one another. While PEACE powers are familiar, you may not be accustomed to thinking of them as power because of what you have experienced and learned in the traditions of the hierarchical power-over model. The PEACE powers are familiar because they are so central in the private world. They are not generally thought of as power because they are not yet the predominant modes of action in the world at large—both public and private. Even though the PEACE powers may seem idealistic when you read about them, when they become visible through action, they create dramatic changes—they become very real.

The PEACE powers and power-over powers are not opposites, but they do contrast sharply. Power-over traits and practices are listed in the left columns that follow. Features and practices of PEACE powers are in the columns on the right, with a focus on the values, as well as the processes through which they are translated into action.[5]

Power-Over Powers

The *Power of Results* emphasizes programs, goals or policies which achieve the desired results. Achievement of the goals justifies the use of any means: "I don't care how you do it, just get the job done."

The *Power of Prescription* imposes change by authority; vested interests prescribe the outcome. The attitude is paternalistic: "Do as I say, I know what is best for you."

The *Power of Division* emphasizes centralization, resulting in the hoarding of knowledge and skills by the privileged few: "What they don't know won't hurt them."

PEACE Powers

The *Power of Process* emphasizes a fresh perspective and freedom from rigid schedules. Goals, programs and timetables are used as tools, but are less important than the process itself.

The *Power of Letting Go* encourages change emerging out of awareness of collective integrity; leadership inspires a balance between the interests of each individual and the interests of the group as a whole.

The *Power of the Whole* values the flow of new ideas, images and energy from all, nurturing mutual help networks that are both intimate and expansive. The sharing of knowledge and skills is viewed as healthy and desirable.

Power-Over Powers	*PEACE Powers*
The *Power of Force* invests power for or against others and is accomplished by a willingness to impose penalties and negative sanctions. One individual makes decisions on behalf of another individual or group of individuals: "Do it or else."	The *Power of Collectivity* values the personal power of each individual as integral to the well-being of the group. A group decision where each individual has participated in reaching consensus is viewed as more viable than a decision made by any one individual and stronger than a decision made by a majority.
The *Power of Hierarchy* requires a linear chain of command where layer upon layer of responsibilities are sub-divided into separate and discreet areas of responsibility: "I don't make the decisions, I just work here." Or "The buck stops here."	The *Power of Unity* shares the responsibility for decision-making and for acting upon those decisions in a lateral network. This process values thoughtful deliberation and emphasizes the integration of variety within the group.
The *Power of Command* requires that leaders are aggressive and followers are passive; leaders are assigned titles, status and privilege (and higher pay!): I will tell you what to do." Or "Tell me what to do."	The *Power of Sharing* encourages leadership to shift according to talent, interest, ability or skill; emphasizes passing along of knowledge and skills in order that all may develop individual talent.
The *Power of Opposites* polarizes issues. Individual preferences are subsumed by the requirement to make choices "for or against." Language reflects the values of "good versus bad," "right versus wrong": "If you aren't with us, then you are against us."	The *Power of Integration* views all aspects of a situation in context without arbitrary value-laden judgments. In the process of enacting self-volition, the individual integrates the qualities of self-love with love-for-others and acts with respect for each individual's entitlement to self-volition.

Power-Over Powers (cont'd.)

The *Power of Use* encourages the exploitation of resources and people as "normal" and acceptable: "If you don't want to work for what we are willing to pay, then quit. There are plenty of people standing in line wanting this job."

The *Power of Accumulation* views material goods, resources and dollars as "things" to be used in one's own self-interest, as well as items to gain privilege over others: "I worked for it, I bought it, I own it—AND I deserve it."

The *Power of Causality* relies on technology to conquer without regard to the consequences that might be carried over into the future. "Oh, the pill is causing you to retain fluid? Here, take another pill, this will make you lose fluid."

The *Power of Expediency* emphasizes the immediate reward or easiest solution. "Oh, radio-active waste? Let's just ship it somewhere else or dump it in the sea."

PEACE Powers (cont'd.)

The *Power of Nurturing* views life and experience as a resource to be cherished and respected. The earth and all creatures are viewed as important and integral to continued existence on this planet.

The *Power of Distribution* values material resources (including food, land, space, money) as items to use for the benefit of all, to share equitably and according to need. Material goods are valued as a means, not as an end in and of themselves.

The *Power of Intuition* senses which actions to take based on the perceived totality of human experience. While technology is considered to be a resource, it is not elected for its own sake or merely because it exists.

The *Power of Consciousness* considers long-range outcomes and ethical behaviors. Ethics and morality are derived from values that protect life, growth and peace; and from values that are the basis for confronting destructive actions.

11

Power-Over Powers	*PEACE Powers*
The *Power of Xenophobia* (the fear of strangers) rewards conformity and adjustment, looking alike and thinking alike are considered as positive assets. "Be a team player. Don't make waves."	The *Power of Diversity* encourages creativity, values alternative views, and encourages flexibility. The expression of dissenting views is expected and encouraged, and all points of view are integrated into decisions.
The *Power of Secrets* relies on the mystification of the process, agents, and the chain of command. The agent who actually has the power rarely implements the decisions or takes direct action, but assigns the dirty work to someone else: "I'm just doing what I was told."	The *Power of Responsibility* focuses on demystification of the processes and insists on naming and/or being the agent; open criticism and self-criticism is encouraged, motivated by love and protection for the individual and the group.

3

Doing It: Making the Commitment

Have you ever . . .

- Been in a meeting where two people argued for most of the time and nothing ever got done?
- Been at a meeting where you never heard what someone was trying to say because she kept getting interrupted?
- Voted against a motion that passed, knowing that your concerns were serious but never heard or addressed?
- Left a meeting thinking that you were the only one who was dissatisfied?
- Left a meeting and then found out in the hall afterwards what was really going on?
- Left a meeting thinking *"There has got to be a better way?"*

There is a better way. The better way is *Peace and Power* in action. These processes are not a guarantee of totally satisfactory outcomes, nor are they automatic solutions to the dreadful meetings you may have experienced. In fact the methods of *Peace and Power*, if used in a cookbook manner, will certainly fail. *Peace and Power* requires that you and your group actively create, shift, and explore ways to put your values into action.

Creating a better way begins with individuals who consciously choose values consistent with the general values of Praxis, Empowerment for all, Awareness, Consensus, and Evolvement. At the same time, creating a better way means taking personal responsibility for making these values visible through action. You can use the methods of *Peace and Power* without thinking about why, and the processes *will* work to create some improvement over groups that have used power-over methods in the past. However, the processes will become transformative for each individual and the group when several individuals move toward the commitments described in this chapter.

The problems that happen in groups do not necessarily arise from evil intent. More often problems arise from values people have learned about patriarchal power-over relations. When power-over values are translated into action, what typically happens is alienation, advantage for some and disadvantage for others, and individual dissatisfaction.

Throughout the remainder of this book, you will see the ideal of creating a new reality through actions based on the PEACE powers. The starting point is to own the value or values you want your actions to reflect, and to begin practicing actions that reflect those values. The following sections provide specific actions you can practice to begin reflecting values of *Peace and Power*. As you read these suggestions, focus on your own thoughts, feelings, experiences, and what you would like to bring into your life. Think about what each of the PEACE powers would be like if you were to bring this kind of energy and influence to your interactions with others.

THE COMMITMENT OF PEACE AND POWER

A Commitment to the *Power of Process* Means:

Actions	*Words*
• Giving yourself and everyone else in the group the time to attend to a concern or issue that exists for any individual.	• Chullie has a concern that I need to think about—I will call her during the week to get clearer before our meeting next week.

Actions	*Words*
• Letting decisions emerge gradually, realizing that very few decisions are urgent.	• I can wait to make this decision. How do others feel about waiting?
• Inviting everyone in the group to express their ideas or concerns during the discussion.	• Some people have not spoken to this issue yet. Do you have concerns that have not been heard by the group?

A Commitment to the Power of Letting Go Means:

Actions	*Words*
• Moving away from your own vested interests in order for others in the group to express their interests fully.	• I would like to protect personal time and not meet on Sunday. But I am open to knowing how others feel about this issue.
• Supporting others who are new, or learning something new, in their work of taking on something you are already skilled at doing.	• Michelle and I will be going over the bookkeeping system the hour before our next meeting. Would anyone else like to join us and begin to participate in this work?
• Expressing your misgivings or concerns about a situation in the group, but letting the sense of the group prevail when the group needs to move on to something else.	• I have voiced my concern about the expense of this project, and the group is clearly moving toward doing it anyway. I trust the wisdom of the group and seek support in letting go of my fear.

15

A Commitment to the Power of The Whole Means:

Actions

- Placing your own individual needs and interests within the context of the group.

- Seeking ways to do things together to equalize power within group.

Words

- I like to work alone and late at night—I could make posters, or balance the accounts, or update the mailing list.

- Nicole, how about updating the mailing list in your late night time? Making posters is a fun group project, and new members need to learn how to balance the accounts.

A Commitment to the Power of Collectivity Means:

Actions

- Taking into account the interests of every member of the group, including those who are not present.

- Making sure that every concern is carefully integrated into every discussion and decision.

Words

- We will consider this decision tentative until the group in California has also discussed this issue and voices their perspectives on it.

- We have heard Jen's concern about the expenses, and her sense that the group wants to go ahead with the project anyway. I think we should go ahead with the project, but also make a clear plan as to what we will do if the expenses start to mount beyond what we can handle.

A Commitment to the Power of Unity Means:

Actions	*Words*
• Addressing conflict openly and constructively, and in so doing working actively to strengthen the integrity of the group.	• I am distressed because Janie and the publicity group have not explained their plan for this event. You always do a great job, but our not knowing mystifies this important process and we have a principle of unity to demystify what happens here. I would like to have you explain the plan at our next meeting so that we can all understand, and help out where we can.
• Keeping the group's Principles of Unity in conscious awareness as a basis for moving forward.	
• Celebrating values and joys that are shared in common.	• I appreciate that the group did not ignore my concern about the expenses, and feel good about supporting this project because of your response.

A Commitment to the Power of Sharing Means:

Actions	*Words*
• Taking responsibility for leadership and tasks, including things you enjoy doing and can do well, as well as things you would rather not do but that need to be done.	• I will take responsibility for the clean-up after the concert. I would like four people who have not done this before to work with me, because the requirements of the theater are important to learn—we need to keep good relationships with them.

Actions	*Words*
• Encouraging others to join in passing skills and tasks along, by assuming tasks from others.	• Randy, you have had responsibility for the inventory for two years now. I am willing to learn how to do this and begin to assume responsibility in this area this coming year.

A *Commitment to the Power of Integration* Means:

Actions	*Words*
• Listening actively and deliberately to every concern or idea that others bring to the group, and taking active steps to understand and act on others' points of view.	• Suzette, what I hear you saying is that you are losing faith in our ability to complete this project because we seem so scattered. Is this an accurate summary of your concern?
• Taking actions that encourage bringing things together, rather than polarizing them into opposing points of view.	• Since everyone can't be here at any time we have suggested for our regular meetings, how about if we alternate between morning meetings and evening meetings?

A *Commitment to the Power of Nurturing* Means:

Actions	*Words*
• Treating others in ways that convey love and respect.	• Pauli, I deeply admire the strength that you have shown in the face of this difficulty. Thank you.
• Acknowledging that each individual's experience has	• June, I haven't faced the kinds of discrimination you

Actions	*Words*
uniquely qualified her to be where she is at the present.	have. It must tax your persistence and patience to keep trying to help us understand. Just know that when I seem resistant, at the same time I truly seek to know and understand.
• Affirming and rejoicing in the knowledge that each person in the group has power to use, and power to choose how to use it.	• Chris, I am sad to see you leave the group, but at the same time I am happy for your clarity in making such a difficult choice.

A Commitment to the Power of Distribution **Means**:

Actions	*Words*
• Taking actions to overcome imbalances in personal material resources among group members.	• Jan and Leslie and I are able and willing to drive our cars and cover this expense so that all 12 of us can go to the retreat.
• Using resources that are available to the group as a means, not an end.	• Linda is willing to help us out of this tax mess at no charge. Rather than filing taxes for us, let's have her teach at least four of us to do what needs to be done.
• Working to make all resources that are available to the group equally available to all in the interest of the development of the group and each individual.	• We have $200 in grant money to cover travel to do the interviews. How can we use the money to help everyone who wants to participate?

A Commitment to the Power of Intuition **Means**:

Actions	*Words*
• Taking the time to think, feel, and experience the fullness of a situation.	• I have been quiet for the past hour, reflecting on my growing sense that we need to go ahead with this. I am not sure why or how yet . . .
• Taking actions that seem risky when your gut tells you to go ahead.	• I know this is a dangerous time to travel in that part of the world. I just feel that we need to participate in this mission.
• Paying attention to the intuition of others and taking their sense of things seriously.	• Dallas, you are so clear about this even though the rest of us can't quite understand. I think we need to pay attention to your intuition about going ahead.

A Commitment to the Power of Consciousness **Means**:

Actions	*Words*
• Talking about the values on which you are building your actions so that everyone can be fully aware of your intentions.	• I am sharing with everyone all the details about how this works so that everyone can participate to the extent that you are willing and able.
• Exploring with others awareness of feelings, situations, responses and meanings in your experiences.	• I am beginning to see a pattern in how we respond to folks who represent the funding agencies. I would like to put this on the agenda for our next meeting, and I will prepare some ideas and questions for discussion.

A Commitment to the Power of Diversity Means:

Actions

- Stopping to carefully consider another point of view when your immediate response is to reject it.

- Taking deliberate actions to keep yourself and the group open to creating accessibility for others who are different or new.

Words

- Wait a minute! I know I just said I don't agree, but maybe I am missing something here. Ann, talk more about what you are thinking.

- Before we move on, I want to back up because I think that new people are probably confused by what just happened. Would it help for us to explain more about what we just did?

A Commitment to the Power of Responsibility Means:

Actions

- Keeping everyone in the group fully informed about anything in your personal life that might effect the group as a whole.

- Acting to make sure that nothing is mystified, that everything that concerns the group is equally accessible to every member.

Words

- As many of you know, I am dealing with a difficult decision about my future, and I know this distracts me from time to time. Know that I welcome anyone bringing me back to the group if you notice that I seem to have mentally wandered away.

- The theater has strict policies to meet their safety standards. I have prepared a chart that shows everyone what their standards are, and the things we have to do to meet them.

Actions	*Words*
• Actively Checking-in and Closing in a spirit of contributing to the growth and development of the group.	• *Check-in:* I am Peggy. I have just left a difficult meeting at work, but am ready and eager for our discussion. I would like to make sure we discuss the poster design on the agenda tonight.
	• *Closing:* I appreciate Monica's explanation of the theater requirements—that was very helpful to me in understanding why we have to do some of this stuff. Along the same line, I am still confused about the finances, and would like Ann and the finance group to give us more information about that next week to demystify that process more. For my affirmation tonight—I believe in myself and our group.

4

Principles of Unity: Foundations for Building Community

. . . Imagine how it feels to always belong—belong in a diversified community, for it is the diversity in nature that gives the web of life its strength and cohesion. Imagine a time where everyone welcomes diversity in people because they know that is what gives community its richness, its strength, its cohesion. Imagine being able to relax into our connectedness, into a web of mutually supportive relations with each other and with nature. . . . Imagine a world where there was collective support in the overcoming of individual limitations, where mistakes weren't hidden but welcomed as opportunities to learn, where there was no reason to withhold information, where honesty was a given. Imagine a world where what is valued most is not power but nurturance, where the aim has changed from being in control to caring and being cared for, where the expression of love is commonplace.

. . . The very fact that you can imagine these things makes them real, makes them possible.

Margo Adair[1]

Communities are defined by the values, concerns or purposes that the individuals within them share. The phrase "global community" encompasses all who live on the planet earth, but the phrase implies a general concern about the interactive global environment, economies, and politics. When groups of people within a community interact on more personal levels, the values, concerns and purposes

23

that bring them together are more explicit, and also more challenging. Individuals begin to experience firsthand what it takes to reconcile their personal preferences and desires with the preferences and desires of others in the group. Groups that create cohesiveness and that can identify what it is that brings them together as a group *are* a community—meaning that whatever their numbers they share certain values, concerns, or purposes.

Building communities for the future calls for a shift that values both cohesiveness and diversity. Learning to make this shift begins by practicing ways to make the values of unity and diversity visible in action. When your group decides to move toward *Peace and Power* processes, you create a context where individuals actively support one another in learning to make the values of unity and diversity visible in action. The more visible your actions become, the more you will transform your larger community.

Principles of Unity make your individual and group values explicit, and help to guide the actions that flow from those values. Principles of Unity provide a bridge between that which brings people together and that which distinguishes each individual within the group. Principles of Unity provide a grounding from which the group can focus their energies, the ideals toward which the group builds, a guide around which to integrate all individual perspectives in forming decisions, a basis for giving one another growthful criticism, and a foundation for transforming diversity into group strength.

Principles of Unity are statements of mutually shared beliefs and agreements that are formed early in the group's experience together. Although writing them down is important, they are alive—they change and grow as the group grows and changes.

Principles of Unity are the basis for each part of the group's ongoing process. They also provide an introduction and orientation to individuals who are considering becoming a part of the group. New members may contribute valuable perspectives that can lead to shifts and changes in the Principles, but the Principles also form a grounding for stability within the group as membership changes.

The written document that contains the Principles of Unity is kept before the group; each member has a copy and works with it constantly. The document is particularly important as a source for forming constructive criticism (see Chapter 8), and when the group is addressing conflict (see Chapter 9). When each member's copy is almost not readable from the penciled-in changes that emerge over time, it is time to consider making a fresh copy!

BUILDING PRINCIPLES OF UNITY

Peace and Power processes are based on a balance between unity within the group and diversity among individuals. Individuals enter a group with differences in style, personality, beliefs and backgrounds, and with shared ideas about the group. In a group committed to using *Peace and Power* processes, differences ultimately strengthen the integrity of the group, because the group values and acknowledges differences openly and works toward reaching mutual understandings of these differences.

Building Principles of Unity begins with everyone sharing ideas about the group, what interests them in being part of the group, and what they expect from the group. Each perspective is expressed as fully as possible. Then the group begins to identify those ideas around which the group members are clearly unified, and those ideas that represent diversity from which to build common understandings.

Ideally, the group forms Principles of Unity in the first few gatherings. For an existing group that chooses to begin using *Peace and Power* processes, the decision to shift to this way of working together is the first step in forming Principles of Unity, and that decision becomes one of the Principles.

The time invested to form new Principles of Unity or to re-examine existing Principles of Unity is the most valuable time spent in group work. Usually a task-oriented group that will meet regularly for a year or more requires two or three gatherings to form a beginning set of Principles of Unity, and regular times set aside after that to re-evaluate those principles.

There are at least seven components that a group needs to consider in forming Principles of Unity.[2] Each component becomes a section of the written document, but the specific Principles will vary according to the needs and purposes of each group.

Who Are We?

The name of a group implies a great deal about the group. You may need to define some words in your name to be clear about your identity. For example, the word "radical" in a group's name might be defined as "fundamental; going to the root." The definitions clarify who you are and who you want to be.

The group may also need to make an explicit agreement about who the individuals within the group are or will be in the future. For example, a group formed to create and maintain a women's center in the community may deliberately seek participation from a broad base of women in the community, including women of color, women of all sexual orientations, women of differing economic classes, etc. A group that is working on the rights of lesbian mothers may actively seek the participation of non-lesbian mothers and also lesbians who are not mothers.

An important dimension of defining membership is getting clear on how open the group is to integrating new members, when, and how this will happen. A group formed to accomplish a specific, detailed and long-term task may need to initially limit membership to a few members who are able and willing to remain dedicated to the accomplishment of the task. While many groups will choose not to be "closed" groups in relation to membership, there may be times when the group needs stability in the membership, and the group might be open to new members only once or twice a year. Making a specific agreement about how long group membership will remain stable is helpful in preventing misunderstandings within the group, and in communicating with others who are not group members.

What Are Our Purposes?

Defining who the group is provides a start in identifying the group's purposes. A women's center group may have the immediate purpose of finding a space, but then they need to identify the purposes for which that space will exist and how it will be used. If one purpose is to provide shelter for battered women, there are additional things to be defined in relation to this purpose, such as whether or not to offer counseling, economic, legal or educational services as well.

Consider your group's purposes in light of what is realistic. The members of a battered women's support group may want to see the group offer a full range of services to women and their children. However, the resources of the group may be such that the initial purpose needs to be limited to fund-raising and educational work. Being clear at the outset about the limits of the purpose can help the group to use their resources and energies in productive ways, rather than in working at cross-purposes.

In each of the following sections, the examples of Principles of Unity are from the Friendship Collective, whose purpose was to study the experience of female friendship among nurses.[3]

What Beliefs and Values Do We Share Around Our Purpose?

Whatever the group defines as its purpose will direct the group toward exploring various values and beliefs related to that purpose. Certain values are fundamental to *Peace and Power* processes; stating these values is important to help each member of the group grow in understanding the meaning of these values. Having the beliefs and values stated provides a way for the group to examine how the values create changes in actions and group interactions.

The beliefs and values that formed Principles of Unity for the Friendship Collective were:

- We believe that friendships among women are fundamental to female survival and growth.
- We value all forms of friendship between women.
- We value our own friendships among ourselves and are committed to living our friendship with deliberate awareness, examining and creating our experience as we go.

What Individual Circumstances or Personal Values Do We Need to Consider as We Work Together?

Consider personal values of all the individuals who are in the group. Different circumstances create different expectations and commitments. Different personal circumstances and experiences also influence what individuals need from a group to feel safe to speak, to act, and to Be.

Women who are single parents or who care for older adults may need careful limits on time and other personal resources. Women who have been verbally abused may need an agreement from group members that people will be careful about how loudly they speak, and take care not to use sarcastic or assaultive voice tones. A person in a wheelchair not only needs space that is accessible, but also needs the group's awareness of the particular fears and challenges faced by someone in a wheelchair. A person who suffers from fat oppression may not need specific physical arrangements, but needs the group's awareness of the discriminations she experiences and how the group can overcome these. Any person who is a "minority" within a group, whether based on race, age, gender, ethnicity, sexuality, social class, education or any other basis, needs recognition and valuing of these differences. Once the group has openly explored the range of personal circumstances of each person's life related to the group's work, then the group can agree on a common set of expectations that everyone values.

Examples of Principles of Unity formed by the Friendship Collective that grew out of personal circumstances and individual values were:

- We will not intentionally take any action individually or collectively that exploits any individual within the group or any other women, particularly exploitation that could arise from our roles as teachers or students.

- We will keep at a minimum any financial expenses needed from any individual in relation to our work and will openly negotiate these demands as they occur.

- We will be conscious of helping one another maintain a balance between the demands of our group work and our personal lives.
- We will maintain careful time limits for our gatherings that each member of the group mutually agrees upon at each gathering.

What Do We Expect of Every Member?

Time, energy, and commitment expectations can take many different forms. For example, group members might be expected to attend a monthly meeting and contribute to the work of a task group that meets about three hours each week. For another group, members might be expected to attend a yearly meeting and work on one project of her choosing during the year. Large groups that do not meet together but join in a network to promote communication might simply expect that every member contribute financially to the network, with the work of specific tasks done by smaller groups as they volunteer to assume the responsibility.

Bring to conscious awareness ways in which you expect each member to interact within the group. You have probably entered groups with an unspoken ideal or hope that everyone will be "open and honest." In reality, most typical groups have hidden agendas and mystified processes. Making expectations clear is one step in the direction of nurturing openness and honesty.

Examples of Principles of Unity that grew out of the Friendship Collective's expectations for interactions were:

- We will meet once a week until the initial stage of the project is planned, and at regular intervals after that we will re-negotiate the frequency of our meetings.
- We will take time to relax and play together.
- We are committed to using *Peace and Power* processes, including making decisions through consensus and learning to provide constructive, growthful criticism for one another.

- We will address conflicts, feelings and issues between us openly as soon as they reach our awareness, with the understanding that early awareness may not be perfect but deserves expression.
- We will share skills, leadership and responsibility within the group according to ability and willingness, and will work to nurture these abilities in each of us so that we share them as equally as possible.
- We welcome any individual assuming specific tasks that need to be done that grow out of our mutually agreed upon direction, and support her initiative in doing so. We expect that each of us will keep every other member of the group fully informed as to the progress of her activities related to the group's work.

What Message Do We Wish To Convey To The Community Outside Our Group?

Every group conveys a message to their larger community about who they are and what they are all about. Sometimes the message is accurate to the intents of the group, other times it is not. In a group using *Peace and Power,* the group forms the message with careful and deliberate intent, and constantly examines the ways in which they are conveying that message. The message that the group seeks is always consistent with what the group believes and values, but there are still choices to be made in relation to that message.

For example, a group that exists to develop services for battered women may decide to form a message that emphasizes women as physically strong, powerful, and resourceful. Another component of that message might be that women help other women, providing support and assistance in a variety of ways. These two messages become central in considering ways in which members of the group interact outside the group. These messages would grow out of the beliefs the group has about women in general, and also beliefs about women who are battered.

Principles of Unity: Foundations for Building Community

Examples of Principles of Unity that the Friendship Collective formed in relation to our message were:

- We will work to form a message that is consistent with what we believe about female friendship and about feminist praxis.
- All public presentations will reflect our cooperative style of working, and will reflect our commitment to share skills, leadership and responsibility.
- We will carefully and constructively criticize each public presentation or written document to examine the message we think we actually conveyed, and to re-form our own commitments and our presentation style as needed to more closely convey the message that we intend.

How Will We Protect The Integrity of Our Group?

Groups often encounter demands for their time and attention from outside the group, particularly when you are doing work that is creating social change. These demands may place unrealistic burdens on the group, and they may not always be consistent with the direction that the group wishes to take. Conscious awareness and anticipation of these possibilities helps a group to develop agreements that can guide responses to outside demands. For example, a group that has been successful at fund-raising might be asked to share their experience and knowledge with another new group in the community. If this happens once, it would not be a burden. But if it happens often, the group's energy could be drained responding to these requests.

Examples of Principles of Unity formed by the Friendship Collective to protect group integrity were:

- All requests of our group will be discussed in a gathering with all of us present, and all decisions made regarding outside demands will be made by consensus of the group.
- Decisions about outside requests will be informed by a primary concern for the protection of each of us individually, our primary commitment to the work of our group, and our readiness to respond to the request.

- We will maintain our commitment to feminist praxis and to feminist methods in our work, and will carefully examine all situations that might result in an erosion of this commitment.
- We will seek external funding for our work, but will examine the demands placed on us in relation to accepting funding to assure that whatever demands these are, they do not compromise our primary principles.

5

Gathering: The Process in Action

Peace and Power processes are alternatives to traditional power structures within group meetings. Moving toward peace processes in conducting a group meeting or gathering helps everyone become clearer as to what the ideals of *Peace and Power* mean. You *see* and *experience* the values in action. When you are not sure if your values and actions are in harmony, you can stop and take a few minutes to discuss why you are doing something. This chapter provides an overview of how a gathering can be conducted using *Peace and Power* processes, and why.

Groups sit in a circle so that everyone has eye contact.[1] Usually one individual, the convener, comes to a gathering with an agenda that provides structure for the gathering. This responsibility rotates among group members at regular times, such as every gathering, or every month. The process for each gathering has several distinct components that encourage each individual to put *Peace and Power* values into practice.

The Convener opens the gathering by beginning Check-In, when each person becomes fully Present—in mind, body, and spirit.[2] Check-In is a time for each individual to focus awareness on the purposes of the gathering, to share with the group any circumstances that might influence participation in the process, and to bring to the group what you expect or hope for this gathering.

Following Check-In, the Convener draws attention to the agenda and begins the process of Rotating Chair (see Chapter 6).

Rotating Chair is a mutually shared responsibility for facilitating group interactions. The "chair" refers to whoever is speaking. The primary purpose of Rotating Chair is to promote every viewpoint being heard, with *each* person's unique contribution being valued and necessary.

Group decisions are reached by Consensus (see Chapter 7). Consensus focuses on reaching a conclusion that takes into account all viewpoints and one that is consistent with the group's Principles of Unity. In contrast to compromise, which is a decision that focuses on what each individual gives up, consensus is a process that focuses on what each individual and the group as a whole *gains* by the nature of the decision that is reached.

The final component is Closing, which is a deliberate process to end a gathering or discussion, and at the same time, begin movement toward the next stage of the group's process (see Chapter 8). During Closing, each person shares *appreciation* for something that has happened during the process of the gathering, *critical reflection* leading toward growth and change, and an *affirmation* that expresses personal commitment for moving into the future.

THE CONVENER

The one individual who comes to a gathering with a specifically defined role is the Convener. A different individual volunteers to convene each gathering so that the task rotates and each person develops leadership skills.

The Convener's primary responsibilities are to prepare the agenda for the gathering, to begin Check-In, and in some types of gatherings, present a SOPHIA (described later in this chapter). During the gathering, the Convener assumes a leadership role, facilitating attention to the mutually agreed upon agenda. The Convener actively listens to the discussion and calls for shifts in the process to facilitate staying focused on what the group's purpose is for this gathering. For example, when the Convener notices that some people have not had an opportunity to speak, she might request a Circling process (see Chapter 6) to give everyone a chance to speak. Or, when she senses that all viewpoints have been heard, she begins the process of decision-making by Consensus (see Chapter 7).

The agenda can be written on a chalkboard or large sheet of paper (shelf liner or freezer wrap will do!) and posted before the time the gathering is scheduled to begin. The Convener also identifies announcements or items that need to be mentioned without discussion and presents these just after Check-In.

Other members of the group can assume leadership roles at any time, but the Convener remains particularly attentive to group movement. This does not mean that the Convener behaves like the traditional "Chairman of the Bored"—calling time limits, reminding people to use Rotating Chair, or calling on people to speak. Once the discussion begins, the Convener is free to participate in the discussion using the process of Rotating Chair (see Chapter 6), just as any other member of the group. Members of the group may also assume leadership.

The Convener's unique responsibility is to make conscious choices to provide leadership and to come to the gathering prepared to do so. Providing leadership that is focused on group process means:

- Letting the group know when agreed-on time limits are near.
- Remaining conscious of requests made by individuals for shifts in the agenda, tasks, or processes, shifts, and making sure these are integrated.
- Helping the group to be aware of alternative possibilities throughout the discussion, such as minority viewpoints that have not received full attention, hearing from people who have not spoken to an issue, or choices that have not been considered by the group.
- Suggesting group processes that can move the group along, such as calling for "Circling" or "Sparking."
- Remaining attentive to possibilities for developing consensus, and providing leadership for the group to do so.
- Shifting the focus of the discussion to closing so that the group has the time they agreed upon for this part of the process.

The following guidelines are for conveners to use in thinking about and planning for gatherings:

Review the Notes from the last gathering:

- Are there items from other gatherings that need to be addressed or items that the group decided to carry over to the next gathering for discussion?
- Are there any new resources needed to enhance the discussions of the items brought forward from the last gathering?
- Has anything happened that will effect the decisions made at the last gathering?

Review Group Process:

- What individual concerns or needs have been expressed that should be considered in planning for this gathering?
- What group issues have people identified that need to be considered in planning for this gathering?
- What group strengths do we have that need to be sustained and supported during this gathering?

Plan the Agenda:

- What announcements need to be shared?
- Are there special time considerations or individual needs to be taken into account?
- What new items need to be introduced?
- What specific tasks or responsibilities need to be done before the gathering?

SOPHIA

In groups where discussion is a primary focus, a SOPHIA can be prepared by the Convener in advance of the gathering, and presented after Check-In and after the group has agreed to the revised agenda for the gathering. A SOPHIA is a 5- to 10-minute verbal essay that comes from the speaker's own inner wisdom. *Sophia* is a Greek word for female wisdom; she was wisdom in ancient western theologies.[3] In the context of discussion groups, a SOPHIA means:

Speak
Out,
Play
Havoc,
Imagine
Alternatives

A SOPHIA is intended to focus the group's attention on the topic of discussion. A SOPHIA is particularly useful in a classroom setting, a book discussion group, when a group is facing an important decision, or when a group is in a muddle about Principles of Unity. If the group has shared readings in advance of the discussion, the SOPHIA draws on those readings, but brings the perspective of the speaker to interpret possible meanings of the readings for individuals and the group. An important purpose of a SOPHIA is to raise questions for all to consider. The questions are also called "subjectives" (not traditional "objectives"). Subjectives are critical questions that arise from varying perspectives on the issue under consideration. There are no answers to subjectives, rather, there are many possible responses, all of which will be respectfully considered in the discussion. The SOPHIA, and the subjectives that it contains, offer to the group many possibilities to consider.

CHECKING IN

Check-In is:

- Calling your name as a symbolic gesture of placing your Self into the circle, fully present in mind, body and spirit.

37

- Sharing circumstances or events that are likely to influence your participation during the discussions.
- Reflecting briefly on what you integrated or gained from the last gathering.
- Saying what you are prepared to contribute to the group interaction and what you hope for the group during the gathering.

Check-In is time for the group to hear every individual speak. Check-In usually opens the gathering to assure that concerns of everyone present are fully considered throughout the group time. Enough time needs to be provided so that each individual speaks, but each person only speaks for a brief time so that everyone's presence is acknowledged before any discussion begins. Check-In is initiated by the Convener and is an indication to all that the gathering has begun.

Check-In is a brief statement by each individual that centers the attention of the group on the shared purpose for being together. By sharing your specific expectations for the gathering, everyone present can integrate these into the whole of the gathering. Once this is done, there are no hidden agendas.

If you are joining an established group, Check-In can feel intimidating. A lifetime of hierarchical group processes creates doubts about how safe any space really is. Until you feel comfortable in a group you may only wish to share who you are and your purpose for being present.

One purpose for "checking-in" is to address your own ability or limits in participating during the gathering. If you are not sure how fully present you are able to be, you might say "I am distracted tonight, but I want to hear the discussion and participate as much as possible." You may choose to provide some details that will facilitate the group's understanding, such as "My dog got out of the yard today and I have not found her. I do have friends searching, and it is important to me to be here and help plan the opening of the Center." It is important to say something about what you hope for by being present. Knowing the circumstances that are influencing your ability to attend to the work of the group, and what you are working for on behalf of the group, the group can respond in a supportive and caring way.

Here is an example of how to share your reflections on a previous gathering to acknowledge what has happened, without imposing on other's time for Checking-In. Suppose that during Closing at the end of the last gathering, comments were shared about Sally's constructive way of responding to another person. Sue reflected on the constructive approach that Sally used and practiced the approach at home. During Check-In, Sue briefly relates what happened and shares with the group that if the situation had not been examined during Closing she would not have been able to change to a more constructive way of dealing with similar situations at home. By Sue's sharing this experience of her own growth, the group can better appreciate the far-reaching influences of their collective actions.

While every individual's Check-In differs in extent and detail, it is vital for everyone to share their intention for each gathering. Silence during Check-In leaves others wondering what you are thinking, and leaves room for doubts about your intents. Silence at this time interferes with creating a safe space. If you cannot participate with a spirit of owning your part of responsibility for the group process, then it is time to Check-Out of the group.

Responding To Check-In

Check-In does not occur in a vacuum. The group briefly focuses energy, time and attention to what individuals share. When a person shares exciting good news, let your congratulations and shared joy erupt! When a person is preoccupied with some circumstance that may interfere with her participation ("my dog is lost"), the group may ask "How can we best respond right now" to find out what the person needs from the group. If someone shares a dramatic and important event—such as the death of a friend—the group may wish to suspend the agenda entirely or alter the agenda in some way.

CHECK-OUT

There are at least two types of Check-Out. First, if you are not able to participate in the gathering in an active way, it is wise to Check-Out entirely—either from this gathering or from the group altogether. Sleeping or reading a book during a gathering does not constitute being present or participating!

Another kind of Check-Out occurs when you are present and committed to the group but you have specific limits on your time and energy for this particular gathering. If you come to a gathering and have to leave before closing, then explain your situation during Check-In and give the time frame you are committed to. As the time nears, request the chair and share any closing comments. Give the group time to attend to your concerns, unfinished business, or to make plans for finishing something you might be involved with.

For example, a gathering has been scheduled to end at 10:00 PM. Neva wants to leave the meeting at 9:00 PM because she is taking an exam the next morning and needs to get a good night of rest. Neva has been involved in planning for a concert that the group is sponsoring and wants to be present for that discussion. She shares her circumstance with the group and requests that the discussion about the concert be placed earlier than planned on the agenda so that she can be present for it. The group agrees to this priority and the gathering proceeds. As 9:00 PM draws near, Neva requests the chair and shares with the group that she is concerned that there are still some loose ends related to the concert. The group shifts attention to Neva's comments, wraps up the loose ends and wishes her the best on her exam.

6

Turning It Over: Rotating Leadership and Responsibility

Rotating Chair is truly "turning it over." Using Rotating Chair turns upside-down the long-accepted custom of hierarchical structures—a linear chain of command where a single individual or an elite group assumes leadership and control. Rotating Chair turns over to each member of the group the rights and responsibilities for leadership, tasks, and decisions.

The process of Rotating Chair may initially seem awkward, cumbersome, inefficient, and a frank nuisance. It is especially tedious to attempt to learn this process by reading. (You are fortunate if you can also learn in an oral tradition!) Once you experience the entire process in the context of a group with mutual intent and commitment to the values of *Peace and Power,* fears and reservations about the process gradually disappear. In fact, it becomes excruciating to try to endure the old ways when you have to go back and deal with the world at large.

ROTATING CHAIR

Rotating Chair is a mutually shared responsibility for group participation and interaction. Whoever is speaking is the Chair. Following Check-In, the Convener focuses on any announcements. The group then reviews the agenda and identifies any items that need to be included that are not on the agenda, or re-orders the agenda based on what people shared during Check-In. If anyone has a brief item that simply consists of information sharing, this is a good time to do so. The group may set time limits and priorities on the agenda items.

In discussion groups, the Convener then shares a SOPHIA. The subjectives (questions) at the end of a SOPHIA often spark discussion. In task-oriented groups, the Convener focuses the group's attention on the first item of business. Then the Chair rotates to whoever wishes to speak and discussion begins. The Chair continues to rotate to members of the group who wish to speak.

Once the discussion begins, you express your desire to speak by raising your hand. The person who is speaking is responsible for passing the chair to the next speaker. You pass the chair by calling the name of the person you are recognizing. If more than one person wants to speak, pass the Chair to the person who has not spoken or who has not spoken recently—*not* the person who raised the first hand.

Passing the Chair by calling a person's name is an important tool for a large group to help everyone learn everyone's name. In any size group it is a symbolic gesture that signifies honoring each individual's identity, and respecting the presence of each person. Calling the next speaker's name is also a clear signal that you have finished speaking, and that you are indeed passing the Chair along.

You are not obligated to relinquish the Chair to someone else until you have completed the ideas and thoughts you wish to share. At the same time, you have the responsibility to make way for all who are present to speak to each issue. Avoid making long, repetitive, or unrelated comments that prevent access to the Chair for other people. If you tend to ramble, and you notice that others are not having time to speak, practice getting your thoughts and ideas clear in a journal or in conversation outside the group, and then ask the group to give you specific feedback about how you are doing.

During the discussion, make notes of your own thoughts and ideas about what others are saying. Listen carefully to people who are speaking, giving way for them to complete their thoughts before you indicate your desire to speak. Frantically waving your hand in eagerness to share your thought is just as distracting and disrespectful as verbally interrupting.

At first, raising your hand can make you feel as if you have gone back to kindergarten. The benefits, however, soon become apparent. You can be confident that you will have a chance to speak, that you can complete your thoughts without interruption, and that someone with a louder voice will not intimidate you. Each person who wants to speak is assured of being able to do so. If you have a soft voice, you know that you don't have to shout to get attention. If you are unaccustomed to speaking in a group, you are assured of having encouragement and the time to practice those skills. If you speak slowly, or you often pause to gather your thoughts, you are assured that nobody is going to jump in and grab the attention of the group before you complete what you have to say.

PASSING IT ALONG: NOTES AND MINUTES

Everyone who participates in a gathering takes notes. These notes facilitate the process of Rotating Chair. They are not a record of the meeting and are not generally shared with the group. They are used as a personal tool to remain in touch with thoughts you have while others are speaking. Your own notes make it possible for you to hold on to an idea that you want to share, without interrupting someone else who is speaking. They form a personal journal of your experiences in the group. They can also serve as a personal reminder of what it is you have agreed to do! These notes are a valuable resource during Closing, making possible your recall of specific process issues to which you want to speak.

For task-oriented groups, at least one individual can assume the responsibility for recording the proceedings of the gathering in the form of Minutes. For gatherings that last longer than about an hour at a stretch, it is helpful to share this task among different individuals in the group. Other kinds of groups may or may not decide to have group minutes.

Minutes are not required, but you may want to keep them for several reasons:

- Minutes provide a permanent record for the group's archives.
- Minutes communicate information to those who are not present at the gathering, so they can be informed of what happened.
- Minutes provide a reference for the Convener of the next gathering, and
- Minutes help those with short memories figure out what they are supposed to do next!

Some groups keep detailed records of all ideas and comments, including who spoke, and a summary of what was said. Other groups keep simple records of who was present at the gathering, the decisions made, and the major factors that contributed to each decision. The group's needs may even vary from one gathering to the next.

TASK GROUPS: GETTING THINGS DONE

Sometimes the *group* (not any individual) rotates responsibilities to a committee, Task Group, or individual within the group. This is common when ongoing tasks require intense work and ongoing attention. The group determines the responsibilities of the Task Group and provides guidelines that help that Task Group accomplish their work in concert with the group's Principles of Unity. The Task Group then decides and acts in accordance with their responsibility. The Task Group brings back to the larger group an accounting of their work and determines issues that require a larger perspective.

One benefit of having Task Groups for specific or ongoing work is the passing along of skills. A Task Group usually gets involved in doing intensive work that requires special skills and knowledge. Learning a skill is accomplished by participating in the work, not by simply hearing about the results of the work. Hearing a finance Task Group's report, no matter how detailed, does not help anyone learn how to balance the books.

Task Groups that are most effective in getting the job done *and* in passing along skills are those that have a balance of people who are experienced at the task and those who are learning. This requires a gradual shift over time in who is involved with any Task Group, so that the work and responsibility rotates.

ACTIVE LISTENING

Active listening is a vital part of the process of rotating responsibility. Active listening means being fully tuned in to a speaker, and verbally checking out your perceptions of what you heard. It requires deliberate awareness of how you perceive what other people say. When you are ready to confirm what you have heard, request the Chair, and paraphrase in your own words what you understood. The speaker can affirm your perception, or clarify any misunderstanding. Other people in the group can also contribute to clarifying the intended message.

THE TYRANNIES OF SILENCE AND REPETITION

Working effectively together is difficult, if not impossible, if some people in the group consistently choose to not speak to issues. Silence, when your viewpoint has not been expressed, deprives the group of the benefit of a viewpoint that they might not otherwise take into account. Silence also leaves people wondering what you are really thinking, or even worse, making assumptions about your thoughts and opinions.

Remember, this process does not function on the notions of "majority" and "minority." Even if you are the only one who holds an opinion, the group must consider this in decision-making. *Every* viewpoint is considered regardless of how many or how few hold that viewpoint. Even more important, *Peace and Power* processes are based on valuing each individual and others can only know what you uniquely offer to the group when you share your opinions, thoughts, and ideas.

At the same time, it is not necessary for every individual to address every issue. If your viewpoint has already been expressed, you need not repeat what someone else has already said, although it is often important that you indicate to the group that you agree with what someone else has already said. If you agree but have a different thought or concern to add, you need to speak to have your additional thought considered in the discussion.

SHIFTING TO "EVERY-LOGUE"

When two people are together, dialogue is highly desirable because it is important for each person to contribute to the discussion—otherwise, it is not a discussion. In a group larger than two, the same principle holds—*everyone* needs to contribute to the discussion—otherwise, it is not a discussion. In a group of more than two people, dialogue is like a monologue in a two-some—one or two people dominate the discussion so that other voices are not heard. Any form of domination in a group discussion models the power-over tactics of traditional meetings. Monologue or dialogue in a group alienates other participants, promotes argument and debate between individuals, and prevents other viewpoints from being heard. Rotating Chair requires "every-logue," assuring that every person speaks with a sufficient balance of time devoted to being heard.

When two people become engaged in energetic opposition to one another's positions, it is especially appropriate to have other voices heard. Conflict can be growthful and desirable (see Chapter 9), but when two individuals in conflict get caught up in the conflict itself, others in the group cannot participate in the discussion. As other people speak, the group can define what the issue really is. Also, the two people who are in conflict have an opportunity to reflect on their own positions, hear the thoughts and feelings of other group members, and decide if their thoughts and feelings are helping or hindering group process.

Sometimes one or two individuals have specific information

about a certain issue. Directing a question to an individual and engaging in information exchange is different from exclusive dialogue. Information exchange is simply that—information exchange. The pitfall to watch for is when a group consistently defers to one or two individuals as the "knowledgeable ones." This is a signal that sharing of information and skills is not happening, and the group needs to give attention to providing the opportunity for everyone to share their points of view or information.

VARIATIONS

Rotating the chair can be done in many different ways, and you will create ways not included here. The idea is to find ways that are effective in expressing the values and intents of *Peace and Power*. Variations are often needed when the group is small (fewer than 6), or large (more than about 35). Small groups tend to be less formal, and often rely on "dinner table" styles of discussion. When this happens, everyone gets to speak, but the discussion may wander. In large groups, some people may not have the opportunity to speak and shy people may find it very difficult to speak.

The following are variations that you can use beyond what you have read about so far.

Sparking

When an issue or a topic generates a great deal of excitement in the group, the discussion often moves naturally into a style that reflects the high energy of excitement. Many individuals begin to speak, sometimes at once, often tossing words and ideas into the air like a fountain.

This type of discussion is known as Sparking. When it begins to happen naturally, let it happen if the discussion is giving the group new ideas and energy to move forward. Once some individuals begin to lose interest, or the ideas are beginning to be repetitive, it is time for the Convener or another group member to assume leadership, asking the group to cease Sparking and return to the more focused style of Rotating Chair.

You can bring an idea or topic to the group that needs Sparking. Ask the group to enter this style of discussion for a specific time, or plan to include Sparking around the idea at a future gathering.

Sparking is a valuable process for creating ideas and energy, but it does not work well to help everyone participate equally, or to be heard. When you use it, do so with deliberate intent, and make sure everyone in the group is aware that this is what is going on. When it is time to cease, you can use Circling as a transition back to Rotating Chair.

Circling

Circling is a time when the group suspends open discussion and rotation of the chair, and *everyone* in the group takes a turn around the circle to speak to an issue. People listen to one another in turn. Nobody responds or discusses any comment or idea until everyone has spoken. If you have questions or want clarification, make a note to yourself so you can seek clarification after everyone has been heard. Although it is usually the Convener, any group member who perceives that the group needs to focus and clarify may request the group to Circle. Whoever calls for a Circle then shares her perception of what the focus of the Circle needs to be.

Everyone speaks very briefly, with comments limited to the focus for which Circling has been requested. This provides a connection with all of the points of view at that point in time. It also provides a few moments for each individual to get clearer before speaking. Even if you have nothing specific to contribute at this time, it is important for you to speak during Circling. You might say: "I am not clear about this issue and need more time."

When the discussion seems to be nearing time for consensus but this is not yet clear, someone can request a circle to simply find out if people feel ready to form consensus on the issue. At the end of Sparking, Circling can be a time for everyone to share which of the ideas expressed "sparked" the most.

A circumstance when Circling is especially helpful is when tensions are running high, with two or three individuals at the center of the struggle. Circling may be used to interrupt exclusive dialogue that often begins during times of tension. Circling gives every individual in the group the responsibility and the opportunity to speak, to share insights of the moment, or to express feelings that may not already be apparent. Circling provides the opportunity for people at the center of the struggle to listen attentively to the perspectives that others have to offer, and time to do some inner work with respect to the struggle.

Circling can be used to begin the process of bringing closure to an issue. Everyone shares ideas about the issue before ending the discussion and moving to another agenda item, to Consensus, or to Closing.

Timing-Call

Despite the best of intentions, individuals sometimes do get carried away speaking to an issue. If a group is having difficulty with extended "mini-speeches" that interfere with everyone having the opportunity to speak, they can agree to use a Timing-Call signal to help speakers remember to bring their comments to a close so that others can speak. A Timing-Call signal is a simple "T" formed with the hands.

A conscious decision to use a Timing-Call signal avoids slipping into unconscious patterns of interacting. Outshouting, long tirades, or other verbal forms of domination are common power-over habits that many well-intended people have cultivated. When a group is using Rotating Chair, a common unconscious habit used to try to interrupt long-winded speakers is hand-waving to ask for the chair while the speaker is still speaking. Not only is hand-waving disrespectful to the speaker, it is disruptive to the process and to the group, and places the responsibility for "monitoring" another speaker on those who are prone to also speak.

When a group recognizes that long-winded speeches are interfering with their process, then a consciously chosen signal is a respectful way to begin to shift patterns of response to others in the group. The Timing-Call signal does interrupt the speaker, but it has several features that are different from the power-over verbal interruptions or the distracting hand-waving technique. It is a signal that is preferably agreed-upon by the group because they share a desire to equalize access to discussion. It is also a signal that is quiet—it does not tend to unnecessarily escalate emotions in the group with loud sound or frantic movement. Importantly, it is a signal that simply reminds the speaker of an agreed-upon responsibility to give way for others to speak. The person who gives the Timing Call is not trying to over-take the speaker by asking to speak. The Timing Call is not a signal requesting the chair; it is simply a reminder to the speaker that it is time to stop talking and give others the opportunity to speak. If no one shows a desire to speak, it is still beneficial for the group to remain silent for a few moments so that everyone can "recover" from the concentration given to the previous speaker and think about the direction they wish the discussion to take. If you are the one speaking when someone gives the Timing Call, you have several benefits: you have an opportunity to re-assess the direction your lengthy comments were taking and re-focus on the group as a whole. If you have become somewhat strident, you can take time to calm down.

Calming the Air

Another hand motion that you can use is a calming motion, sometimes using both hands, palm down, moving in a slow circular motion as if you were petting a cat. This motion is very helpful for groups that tend to work with a high level of anxiety and stress, or who tend to erupt into unproductive Sparking types of discussion. Instead of being helpful to the group, frequent eruptions of everyone talking at once is a signal that anxiety and stress are running amuck. As with the use of the Timing Call, a group can benefit from recognizing this pattern in their interactions and deliberately choosing to take steps to change what happens.

The Calming the Air motion reminds everyone of their commitment to change interactions that feed unproductive anxieties, and to change to interactions that help everyone remain focused and calm. When someone calms the air, the group can cease the yelling or talking-at-once, take a deep breath together, and remain still while they gather their thoughts and feelings to address what is going on.

Random Ravings

Sometimes people think of loose ends that were not completely finished during a discussion, or the group leaves a piece of business unresolved for lack of clarity on the matter. At some point during the gathering, usually toward the end, loose ends tend to become more obvious. It is helpful to set aside a few moments for everyone to reflect on any items that may need to be mentioned briefly before the group ends. This time on the agenda is called Random Ravings.[1]

While you make your own notes during the gathering, remember that there will be time for addressing Random Ravings. You can circle any note you want to address later, and not interrupt the flow of the current discussion. When the time for Random Ravings arrives, a quick review of your notes will help you recall these fleeting thoughts. Everyone can scan their notes to see if any loose ends might be dangling that now need to be addressed. If a loose end deserves more discussion, the group can agree to place the item on the agenda for the next gathering.

7

Cooperation and Collectivity in Action: Consensus

Consensus requires active commitment to group solidarity and group integrity. Arriving at a decision by Consensus while taking into account all viewpoints on a given issue is no easy task, especially if you are accustomed to voting. However, it is possible. Once you experience decision-making by Consensus, it is one of the most rewarding and growthful components of a *Peace and Power* approach to group process.

Consensus within a diverse group is possible because it is formed within the context of the group's purpose, and is built consciously to be consistent with the group's Principles of Unity. The Consensus-making process, at the same time, contributes to clarifying and revising the purpose of the group and the Principles of Unity.

A group decision reached by Consensus is stronger, more valuable, and more lasting than one achieved by a majority, where (sometimes large and important) minority preferences are not taken into account. A Consensus decision is also stronger than any decision made by an individual, no matter how well-informed that individual. When everyone has participated in shaping a decision, each individual can *act* in concert with that decision because they understand everything considered in reaching the decision.

Voting, which uses and reinforces a divisive "power-over" dynamic within groups, is not used in the Consensus-making process. All opinions, even if only one person brings a particular opinion to the group, are equally valued and carefully considered. As each perspective is considered, it is integrated as an explicit part of the decision, or as a factor that informs the direction the group takes.

Consensus is commonly confused with compromise, but they are very different. Compromise focuses on what each person gives up to be able to live with a decision. Compromise decision-making is often called "consensus" because the group is not voting, but instead trying to agree. In seeking simply to achieve agreement, the group relies on making individual concessions that result in a bottom line on which everyone can agree.

In contrast, Consensus decision-making embraces differences of perspective by individuals, while building unity around the group's purposes. Consensus decision-making is a process that focuses on what each person *and* the group as a whole *gain* by the nature of the decision they reach. The group members share agreement *of purpose* once they make the decision. The group carefully considers individual wishes, preferences, or desires and integrates these considering the group's shared purposes. A Consensus process calls for each individual to shift attention to that which the group as a whole sincerely values as a community, and to participate in decision-making that enhances that shared vision or value. If an individual concedes a personal preference during Consensus building, it is done as an affirmative step to collectively support the group's shared purpose and vision.

Consensus is not totalitarian "group-think." What protects against this *is* the commitment to value and hear dissenting views, and to refrain from making a decision until group members have fully addressed the dissent. The group's Principles of Unity provide a common focus for examining diverse views, but are a guide, not dogma. A new viewpoint on an issue can challenge the group to re-examine their Principles of Unity, resulting in healthy growth and change. Individuals actively voice their diverse ideas about an issue, while respectfully considering all other views and the overall sense of the group. Out of this balance grows an ability to willingly move toward a decision that is best for the group.

At the end of this chapter, an example illustrates the subtle but important differences between compromise and Consensus.

CALLING FOR CONSENSUS

When the group has heard all opinions about an issue, the Convener or another member of the group summarizes what may be the predominant sense of the group and asks if this summary is satisfactory to all who are present. At this point, any alternate viewpoint is expressed and the discussion continues with a focus on reaching a conclusion that takes into account all viewpoints. When there are no new possibilities, the group has reached consensus.

Although the process at times seems unending by encouraging full discussion of controversy and differences, the satisfaction that comes from hearing each individual's thoughts and ideas far outweighs any frustrations. Consensus decision-making is often more "efficient" than other forms of decision-making. This is true because there is rarely misunderstanding about what the group has decided, and people can fully invest in acting on the decision.

If discussion of an issue does not flow easily to decision by Consensus, the group can decide not to decide at that time and leave the issue open for discussion later. Actually, there are few decisions that cannot wait. Having to decide "not to decide" carries its own message: more thought and planning need to go into the matter to form a sound decision.

If a decision seems urgent and the group is unable to reach Consensus, someone needs to call for the group to reflect on how urgent the decision really is. If it is truly not urgent, or if they can make an interim decision, the group leaves the matter open and places it on the agenda for the next gathering. If the decision is urgent, then the group must focus on the necessity of reaching a decision that everyone can live with, and plan for more discussion of the issues involved.

Every member does not need to be present whenever the group makes a decision. For most decisions, those individuals present in a group can reach Consensus at the time the group discusses an issue. This is possible because the group's Principles of Unity guide the process, and all members are clear about the Principles of Unity. However, if the decision being considered is one that directly affects the work of members of the group who are not present, consider the decision as tentative until all individuals who are affected can be part of the discussion. Those present for the discussion are responsible for sharing with those not present the full range of factors considered by the group, either in a written account, audiotape, or discussions with group members. If those who are not present bring new viewpoints to the matter, then the group continues the discussion over several gatherings to assure that everyone has the opportunity to participate in the discussion and in the Consensus-building process.

POSITIVE DISSENT

The ability of an individual or small minority to dissent is a strength that guards against the dangers of totalitarian groupthink. At the same time, dissenting individuals hold enormous potential to act in a divisive power-over manner. If you find yourself in a situation where you or someone else is standing alone or in a small minority to represent a point of view that is at odds with most members of the group, you and the group have special responsibilities to seriously consider exactly what is happening. This is a group issue, and if the group responds constructively you all build skills in valuing diversity. Take care not to dismiss dissent as someone just being difficult.

Reaching a point in the consensus process where positions are polarized is a signal that the group as a whole needs to step away from the "what" of the discussion and examine underlying values and commitments. Again, this means taking time to attend to your processes and this may feel very tedious. However, when you consider the typical alternatives—hurt feelings, misunderstandings beyond repair, broken relationships, resentment and anger that come from unresolved disagreement, taking the time to attend to what is happening in the group seems like a very attractive alternative indeed. At this point you may need to set aside decision-making and move to the processes of conflict transformation (Chapter 9).

Cooperation and Collectivity in Action: Consensus

Consider the following specific questions when you face dissent in making a consensus decision:[1]

Have the people who are dissenting fully disclosed their objections, and the underlying concerns, values and reasons for their objections? Everyone may need to help in placing words around an individual's concerns. Sometimes getting clear about exactly what is motivating dissent is not an easy thing to do, especially when you are in the difficult situation of being alone in your opinion. If you are in the majority, you may not agree with the person who is dissenting—take care not to assume that the dissenters have fully disclosed their concerns.

Have all members of the group fully heard, and do we all appreciate the concerns of those dissenting? One way to affirm the group's solidarity in appreciation of the minority view is to have everyone state the dissent in their own way, and reflect to the group what they might do if this were their own perspective. In other words, have everyone place themselves in the shoes of the dissenting view.

What underlying principle of unity or value does this situation bring to light? The value or principle may not be one that the group has addressed before, and getting clear about a new underlying value can have a major influence on what next step the group takes. If you identify an underlying value that is already part of your group's principles, and this situation is challenging that value, this is a signal that the group may be at a turning point in its growth.

What are all the possible decisions that we could make on this issue, and which of these possible decisions best reflect our group's purpose and our Principles of Unity? Once you have all the alternatives clearly identified, and once you explicitly match the alternatives with what your group is really all about, you are likely to be able to arrive at a decision.

EXAMPLE: DECIDING WHEN TO MEET

This example illustrates the differences between compromise decision-making (where the focus is on what individuals have to concede), and Consensus decision-making (where the focus is on what everyone and the group gains). The decision—when to meet—seems on the surface like a relatively easy and somewhat inconsequential decision. However, this type of decision, like any other type of decision, calls forth the same challenges as any decision, and reveals the values and strengths of the group in building community.

In this example, a group of students who are in a very intensive professional program have formed a support group to study together and to practice the skills they are learning in a safe and supportive context. The demands of their class schedules and personal lives make it very difficult to find a good time to meet, but everyone in the group remains adamant that they want to meet weekly. They all feel that the benefits of the group are essential to their individual well-being, and they have agreed that they are "all in this together" and want to make the commitment to contribute to one another's success in the program.

Compromise:

After some discussion, the group decides to "Circle" to be clear about everyone's preference. Several prefer Wednesday mid-day, during a 90-minute break between classes. Several others prefer Friday afternoon after class. Those who object to Wednesday feel that cramming a group meeting between classes makes the day too long and intense. Those who object to Friday feel that they are too burned out at the end of classes on Friday to be able to participate in the group.

> *Sue:* How about if we rotate days? Then people could participate on the days they prefer.
>
> *Sally:* Then we would really be breaking into two separate groups—I would rather not do that.
>
> *Randy:* Wait a minute. I suggested a possibility—to meet before class on Wednesdays when we are all fresh and not tired. Nobody has paid *any* attention to what I suggested. What kind of group *is* this anyway?

Cooperation and Collectivity in Action: Consensus

The group decides to Circle again to make sure that everyone has considered Randy's suggestion, and to see if people have any other new ideas.

> *Amanda:* Well, it seems to me that most people have spoken in favor of Friday. After all, we will never find a time that suits everyone. Can we just agree to meet Friday for at least six weeks, and then we can change to another time if people want to do that?

Resigned, everyone agrees. In this scenario, the group has actually voted based on the majority not having to give up their personal preference about meeting time. Nobody leaves feeling particularly good.

Consensus:

On the next Friday, the group does meet and everyone is present. During Check-In, several people make clear to the group how burned out and tired they are and how much they wish they could find another time to meet. The agenda was supposed to focus on planning several practice sessions before the mid-term exams. Amanda tells the group she has thought about the time-to-meet issue, and wants to at least share some of her thoughts before they start the agenda.

> *Amanda:* Look, I don't necessarily want to open this thing up again, so if people don't want to discuss this after I tell you my thoughts, that will be fine with me. But what I was thinking is that we need to shift our focus to why we want to do this in the first place—which is to be a support group for one another. We clearly can't all always be here for lots of different reasons, even when we want to be. We just don't want to meet at a time that blocks someone from being able to be here (like when they have to be at work). So what I was wondering is—how can we be a support group for one another but not depend exclusively on when we meet? For example, we have a phone tree—we could use that to pass along words of encouragement and funny jokes—not just announcements about snow days. We could also look at the

time we meet in light of when during the week we feel the most vulnerable and in need of support. And, I think that it would be very supportive if I know when this group meets and where, and what is going to be happening, and so if I want to consider not being there I know what I am missing, and I can always connect with folks who can be there.

Jo: What you are saying makes so much sense, Amanda—and it does fit with something I thought about after our last discussion. I was so turned off by that whole thing that I really began to wonder what kind of support we could be for one another if we can't even decide about when to meet and feel good about what we decided. I was just totally wiped out after that meeting and all I could think about was what on earth went wrong?

Sue: I agree. After our last discussion I realized that I really don't like the idea of rotating the days like I had suggested—Sally was right that then we would break into two groups. I think that having a regular day and time is important because this leaves no question about how to find one another and where, when we really do need to connect.

Sally: Another thing that I think is important is what Amanda said—we all need to know what is going to happen from week to week so we can decide if it is worth being there. I want this group to be meaningful and important—not just a feel-good party time, although I hope we party some! But if I am really tired or stressed out, I need to know what the group is planning to do to make a good decision about making the effort to be there.

Randy: What if only one or two people show up and they really need other people there to help with their practice, but the rest of us have decided that it is not worth our effort to be there? (Everyone pauses while people think about this possibility.)

Stephanie: We could agree that if anyone is going to the meeting knowing they need to practice, and they need others there to give feedback, they let all of us know in class so that the rest of us can realize how important this is tó someone, and plan to go to help one another. After all—to me that is what support means—helping one another and not just getting help for myself. But it would also help me if I know what my friends need.

Melanie: And I do want our time to be productive and worthwhile. I will be very motivated to be there even at a time that is inconvenient for me if I am sure we are all committed to making it worthwhile.

(Everyone pauses again, this time suggesting that they have no additional viewpoints to share.)

Amanda: I've been taking some notes—here's what I have so far: We need everyone to count on when and where the group will meet so we can plan. Everyone needs to know in advance what the topic or activity is going to be. We want to know any individual needs before the group meets when this is possible. We want to make it productive and worthwhile time in terms of supporting one another. Anything else so far?

The group affirms Amanda's summary and makes a few suggestions to refine it. They then decide that they will stay with this Friday time—after all they were all here today and despite being really burned out it turned into a very energizing time together. They decide to re-assess the time at the end of the term, and more importantly, to reflect on how they are feeling about their ability to support one another. They agree that everyone needs to be there for that discussion, and people show a willingness to make that commitment. Stephanie agrees to convene the next meeting and to circulate an initial draft of a plan for practicing so that they can discuss the plan quickly next Friday, and begin practicing their skills.

8

Stepping from Here to There: Closing

Closing is:

- Evaluating the group's effectiveness.
- Gaining self-knowledge and knowledge of the group.
- Strengthening communications within the group.
- Focusing on process rather than product.
- Expressing love and respect for individuals and the group.

Closing is a time when every group member shares thoughts and feelings about what has happened during the gathering, and about what they would like to happen next. Each individual's closing is a three-part statement that includes:

- *Appreciation* for someone or something that has happened during the process of the gathering.
- *Critical Reflection* that brings to the group constructive insights about the processes of the group.
- *Affirmation* that expresses your commitment to moving forward with the group's work and your own individual growth.

Closing a gathering using this process assures that the group remains open to imagining and exploring alternatives, and uses the experiences of the group to form the future. Closing is a process that brings together each individual's intent and commitment, and the group's Principles of Unity. The overall purpose of Closing is to strengthen the group and each individual.

Although Closing is one of the most growthful parts of *Peace and Power,* it initially feels quite risky. Often during Closing, feelings that were undercurrents in discussions during the gathering are expressed openly, something that is not customary in typical groups. Ironically, feelings of caring and appreciation are also usually not expressed because people fear they will be misunderstood or misinterpreted. Angry or hurt feelings are especially avoided because they are simply not supposed to be acknowledged openly. During Closing, group members acknowledge feelings in a constructive way so that everyone in the group can develop a fuller understanding of one another and of the group. When this happens, everyone has the benefit of knowing what is really going on, internally for individuals, and also within the group. When your group practices the skills involved in Closing, you are building an important foundation for the skills of Conflict Transformation (Chapter 9).

THE CLOSING PROCESS

Use the Closing process to end gatherings, or to end a lengthy or intense discussion on a single topic, particularly during a gathering that lasts a day or longer. When the time to close arrives, set the discussion aside, and shift focus to reflection on the group's process. To have the benefit of Closing, everyone who is present at a gathering has to be fully *Present* for Closing.

Sometimes you may be tempted to skip Closing, especially in the early stages of getting established, or when decision-making has consumed your time. This is most unwise because Closing is a process that assures that you and the group will not unconsciously slip into habits and practices that undermine *Peace and Power* values. Once you begin to experience the benefits of Closing, your group will become dedicated to setting aside the time you need at the end of each gathering. One way to estimate the time you need is to plan for each person to have about one minute to speak during Closing. Or, for a one-hour meeting, plan about ten minutes for Closing. For a gathering of a day or longer, set aside an hour or more for closing. At the agreed upon time, the group takes a few minutes for each person to silently reflect on what has happened during the discussion and to review notes of the gathering. Each person then shares appreciation, critical reflection, and affirmation.

Appreciation

Appreciation acknowledges something that someone did or said, or a positive group interaction. It is a brief, but meaningful statement. This is a time to actively nurture one another by sharing your ideas about specific ways in which you and the group benefitted from something that happened. For example, if someone's comment in the discussion was a turning point to help clarify an issue for you, or moved the group discussion to a different level, you would state your appreciation for the comment, and share with the group how or why this comment was so important to you and the group.

An appreciation includes the following elements:

- The names of individuals who are responsible for what it is you appreciate.
- A brief description of their specific acts or behavior.
- Sharing what this means to you.
- Your ideas about what this means in terms of the group's purposes or Principles of Unity.

An example of this type of appreciation is:

"I appreciate your leadership, Amanda, in shifting our focus from our individual wants and needs to our collective purpose. I learned so much by what you did and how that turned our discussion into working so well together. Thank you."

Critical Reflection

Critical reflection (also called criticism), is careful, precise, thoughtful insight directed toward transformation. It is a tool for becoming aware of actions and behaviors that maintain an unjust society. It flourishes as a positive group process when the group also maintains a context of love and respect. When you use criticism with commitment to *Peace and Power* values, you practice a powerful skill to move toward agreement on what will be done and why. By working through disagreements and doubts, a group is better able to remain united and can continue to work together when the going gets tough.

Critical reflection is like criticism in the Arts, where developing your art to its finest level depends upon your own and others' constructive criticisms. This type of criticism identifies the meanings of your work, and reveals what creative possibilities can develop further.

An art critic brings to the art insights and interpretations that help others to appreciate more fully what the artist has done, and what the art means for the culture as a whole. The critic does not proclaim the "correct" view of the art, but does provide a well-informed, knowledgeable interpretation of the art that helps others understand the art better, even if they don't agree with the views of the critic.

In *Peace and Power* processes, the critical reflections you bring to the group represent the best you have to offer, as well as the intent of helping everyone better understand what the group is all about. Use the following guideline, especially when you are learning, to frame your critical reflection so that you claim ownership of your concerns, provide specific and clear content, and do so in a way that is likely to be heard and received by others in the group.[1]

A growthful and constructive criticism includes:

- I am . . . (your own feeling about what has happened).
- When . . . (a specific action, behavior or circumstance that is the focus of your thinking).
- I want . . . (specific changes you want to happen).

- Because . . . (how your concern connects with the group's Principles of Unity).

Later in this chapter, in the "How-to's, Helpful Hints and Homework" section, you will find additional guidelines for framing a constructive critical reflection. An example of this type of statement is:

> I am anxious about the fact that we skipped our discussion to plan for the new member gathering next week. I want at least four of us to meet either after this meeting, or tomorrow, to plan for next week because we are committed to modeling competence and confidence in our work together, and this is especially important when we are presenting our group to possible new members. Sue, Jen, and Amanda—would you, or anyone else, be willing to work with me on this?

Affirmation

The conclusion of the three-step process of Closing is a statement of affirmation that gives the group a sense of the way in which you are working to grow as an individual and as a member of the group. Affirmations are simple statements that speak to your deeper Self. They concentrate your energy on the healing, growthful aspects of your work with the group. They are a powerful tool for creating change and growth in a direction that you desire.[2]

An affirmation reflects a reality that is not yet fully a part of your life, but you state it as if it has already come about. Affirmations offered during Closing grow out of your experiences in the group, and often relate to your specific appreciations and critical reflections. They also come from the internal work you do apart from the group. For example, at a time when you feel uncertain about a decision, your affirmation might be: "I trust my own inner sense and the wisdom of our group." When a conflict has disturbed you, an affirmation to help transform the conflict might be: "I reside in the care that we have for each other."[3]

Initially you may find it difficult to affirm yourself. Until you are comfortable creating your own, use an affirmation that some-one else suggests. As your sense of self-affirmation grows you will create your own. As you become accustomed to using affirmations as a source of directing your energy to create change, you will become skilled at expressing an affirmation during Closing that moves you and the group from the circumstances of the present into a future you choose and create.

The following characterize an affirmation:

- It is a positive and simple statement.
- It is stated in the present tense.
- It is grounded in your present reality, but also provides a bridge to the future you seek.

An example of this type of affirmation is:

I am open to receive the love of the group.

HOW-TO'S, HELPFUL HINTS, AND HOMEWORK

Because Closing is so important, the following sections provide more detailed explanations and suggestions.

Getting Your Head and Heart Together

Getting ready to participate in Closing requires thoughtful reflection so that you are clear about the content of what you want to say before you speak. Once you are clear about the content of your three-part closing statement, you can state it briefly and simply.

You have probably not learned to share your own responses to situations while you are in the situation. If this is the case, don't worry—you are not alone. Doing so does not come easily or naturally. Practice is important. Even more important is a supportive, aware group that is fully committed to each individual's growth.

Written notes that you have taken throughout a gathering are very important at the time of Closing. Productive gatherings are rarely uneventful, and in the intensity of the discussion you are likely to have thoughts and feelings about *what* happened and *how* it was being done. Perhaps your perspective has shifted now that the discussion has ended. You may have become aware of an insight and are beginning to get clearer as the discussion comes to a close. Your notes provide words and ideas that you write as these things happen so that you won't forget, and you can review your inner process when it is time to close. To help get clearer about your thoughts, ask yourself:

- Did I *Do* what I *Know*—were my behaviors consistent with my values and with our Principles of Unity?
- Were my actions honestly motivated by love and respect for myself, others, and the group?
- Did I remain tuned in and aware or did I check-out mentally at some point?
- Am I aware of conflicts or differences that we still need to address?
- What occurred that promoted my own individual growth and the growth of the group?
- What changes would I like to make in my behavior?[4]

Being Specific about the Agent

One of the most familiar, yet subtle power-over powers is mystification, or secrets—actions that obscure responsibility for what happens (see Chapter 2). Sometimes owning responsibility can be uncomfortable because you regret what you are doing or have done. Often it is difficult to own responsibility because of shyness or false modesty. Sometimes you may feel a concern (possibly misguided) about protecting a "confidence." Sometimes people are hesitant to name someone specifically because of fear that you will offend or embarrass the person. Sometimes discomfort comes from a general sense of something that you have not thought through.

To make this shift, consider why it is so important. Naming an instance and an agent(s) (especially when the agent is yourself) is critical for growth to occur. If you don't know what or how to change, you can't take positive steps to do so. When people are obscure and mystify a concern, others can sense that something is amiss, wonder if they are responsible or "to blame," and begin to feel a lack of trust, suspicion and divisiveness. Naming the agent helps everyone in the group to understand more about the context of the issues. It becomes possible for the group to move forward to build trust and trustworthiness because everything is out in the open and everyone knows that no secrets or hidden agendas will be kept.[5]

Consider the following examples:

Mystifying statement: "The checkbook ledger has been well maintained for the past few months. This will make taxes much easier to prepare this year." Although everyone in the group may know who has been keeping the checkbook lately, and who is going to prepare taxes, this statement discounts the individuals and makes them anonymous. It creates divisiveness because of the implied message that someone before had not done a good job of keeping the checkbook (which may not be at all what you are referring to, or which may not be true).

Demystifying statement: "Anne, you have done a wonderful job of keeping the checkbook. I appreciate how much this will help me in getting the taxes prepared." This statement lets everyone in the group know how well Anne, specifically, has been doing her job of keeping the checkbook balanced. It carries the message that Anne has a skill about which others might want to know. It lets everyone know that you own the responsibility for getting taxes prepared, and that you see your task as dependent upon the work that others are doing. The focus on the present situation effectively erases the implied mystifying message about what happened in the past.

Mystifying statement: "I can't stand all this clutter!" Here you are owning the fact that you see the clutter, and that you have some negative feeling about it. The mystification and divisiveness in this statement arises from the fact that each person in the group has to wonder if you are mildly irritated, annoyed, furious, or just what.

They also have to wonder if you meant your remark for them personally, or what they might have done to help bring on this outburst. The matter of the clutter becomes only a vehicle for expressing your feelings, which may be due to the clutter, but also could be directed at a person in the group whom you view as responsible for the clutter. This lack of clarity breeds distrust, suspicion, and divisive power-over relations.

Demystifying statement: "I am irritated with this clutter. I am not sure who is responsible, but it seems to me that it is worse after Jane, Randy and Joan have been here for their publicity meeting. Maybe we need more space to store their art supplies. Or, maybe we are all just getting careless about leaving things around. I am willing to help work out a solution. What do other people think?" Here you state the fact that you are not sure about who is responsible, and your uncertainty is more believable because you go on to identify a group who may be contributing more than others. You are also offering a possible solution, and stating your intention to help solve the problem. This invites discussion and leaves you accessible to the group in the event that they find your compulsion over clutter irritating. You have left no room for suspicion, and trust and cohesiveness can build within the group because of the message that "we are in this together."

Being Specific about Your Feelings and Your Observations

A feeling statement is a precise communication of what is happening within yourself. It carries no hidden messages about what anyone else has done or is doing. An observation statement is a clear description of what you or someone else has done or said. An observation does not include what you think another person meant or what you suppose they intended.

Since owning and expressing feelings is risky, people tend to hint about something that someone else is doing or saying. Labeling a person "arrogant" is a hint that you have feelings about the person. Owning your own feelings of jealousy and competitiveness because she is good at what she does makes your feelings about the person clear. Being clear about your feelings avoids la-

71

beling, blaming, or guilt-tripping another person. It lets other people know what is going on with you in a way that invites more discussion.

Compare the following statements:

Interpretive/blaming statement: "I feel rejected because I am never included in things." Even though the speaker uses the word "feel," this statement avoids the real feelings of anger, annoyance, or hurt and implies what others are doing or not doing. The global phrase "I am never included . . ." invites defensiveness and resentment from others in the group. You may think someone has rejected you because of something that happened, but your feeling is anger, hurt or fear, whatever the intention or behavior of the other person.[6]

Constructive statement: "I am angry because I didn't know about the change in our meeting time." This statement expresses exactly what you are experiencing, states a fact about what has happened, and can lead to a constructive response. The response might clarify a misunderstanding: "I was disappointed that you weren't at the meeting. I expected that you would be there because I left a message tucked in your door Tuesday afternoon. In the future, I will make sure that I get information to you directly."

Interpretive/blaming statement: "Sue, you are so irresponsible." This statement inappropriately assigns a personality trait to Sue. Being labeled "irresponsible" puts Sue in a box without any openings. Your statement is a judgment that merely intimidates Sue and everyone else in the group, creates divisiveness, and cuts off discussion.

Constructive statement: "Sue, I am irritated because you have been 30 minutes late for the last four meetings. When you arrive, the group always gets distracted. I invite some discussion among all of us about things we could do to address this issue." This statement clearly expresses what you are feeling and identifies the behavior that you have observed and how it affects the group. Undoubtedly Sue will feel uncomfortable about having her lateness before the group for discussion. By inviting everyone's discussion, Sue can wait to respond and benefit from having other perspectives. Group members can all enter into a problem-solving discussion without placing Sue in the spotlight, or simply making her feel guilty. In this example, everyone knows Sue is consistently late, but what nobody knows is why, and if something is going on that they all need to address. Once the discussion begins with everyone willing to own part of the problem, Sue can address what circumstances in her life have led to her being late, or she can participate in considering a change of meeting time, or both. If you are tempted not to address the issue because you know Sue might be uncomfortable, consider the alternatives. Your irritation would likely grow and affect your relationship with Sue. If this is also bothering others, Sue will feel something much more uncomfortable directed to her from the group as everyone's irritation grows.

Stating What You Want

When giving criticism directed toward something that needs to be done or that needs to change, provide a clear, specific statement of what you want. Focus on what you *do* want. Stating what you want is not a demand, nor does it mean that the group will respond by giving you what you want. What it does is move the group toward a solution or toward a constructive response to your criticism. If your criticism turns out not to fit for others in the group, the group can sort that out and still attend to your concern.

Typical habits of hierarchical culture lead to two tendencies: stating what you don't want or merely implying what you want with some indirect or non-specific comment. Compare the effectiveness of each of the following statements:

> *Constructive statement of what you want:* "I want two kids to help with this project."
>
> *Saying what you don't want:* "I don't think we should have too many kids on this project."
>
> *Implying what you want indirectly:* "Kids in this group just aren't willing to get involved."

Responding to Appreciation and to Criticism

The most difficult thing to learn about both appreciation and criticism is how to take them. No matter how well delivered, hearing either appreciations or criticisms is not easy, especially in front of a group. When you receive an appreciation, you have the following responsibilities:

- Remain in an attentive listening mode while the person who is sharing the appreciation has completed her thoughts. Do not interrupt or respond directly. Appreciation is shared not only for you to hear, but for the entire group to learn and grow from. Your response would interrupt this process.

- Most often you need only to listen. If you do respond verbally in the group, graciously accept the appreciation. For women especially, discounting compliments or putting them down in some way is typical. People tend to say things like "Oh, it was nothing," or "Well, I could have done it better." These responses discount the person who has shared the appreciation, and detract from the growthful effect that the appreciation, and one's own actions, could have for the entire group.

When you receive a criticism, you have at least four responsibilities:

- Listen actively to make sure you understand clearly what the criticism is. This usually means that your first verbal response is to paraphrase what you perceive the criticism to be.

- Wait to hear the perspectives of others in the group. Usually different people have different perceptions of a situation, and hearing these will help you decide how well the criticism "fits."

- Weigh within yourself how fair or accurate the criticism is. Sometimes you will know immediately that it is fair. More often, you will need a few minutes or several days to reflect on the criticism and integrate it.

- Respond in a constructive manner. For a fair criticism, the most constructive response is a behavioral response—you take the criticism to heart and change your behavior. If you decide that the criticism is not fair, share your thoughts with the group.

Responding to criticism without defensiveness or apologies is difficult and often people don't even recognize these habitual responses. Defenses or apologies do not contribute to the growth of the group, yourself, or other individuals. Compare the following responses:

Constructive response: "I think that you are right, Jane. I will work on being here when our meetings begin. Or if you think the criticism has an element of unfairness: "I don't like being late either. But Jane, you have not taken into account the fact I ride the bus. I am wondering if the group could meet later so that when my bus runs late I won't be late for the meeting."

Defensive response: "I think that Jane is right but I am working as hard as I can to be here." Or, "Give me a break. I'm doing the best I can." If you think that the group has not recognized your contributions, then share this thought with the group but focus on what you are feeling and thinking about your future behavior in relation to the issue of being late.

Apology: "I know that Jane is right and I am very sorry. What more can I say?" You probably could say a lot more to help the group address the issue. You can also *act*—take steps to address the issue yourself. Being sorry does not make things right nor does it help you or the group move forward. If you feel regretful about what happened, share your feeling of regret and suggest what you and the group can learn from the situation.

Putting It All Together

In reading about how to say things constructively, you may have lost sight of how this works together in a group. The following situation provides an example of how a group can work with a critical reflection. This example starts with a critical reflection given at the end of a gathering, when Justa became increasingly aware of the ageist implications of a remark she made in response to Adrienne, a younger woman in the group. At the time of Closing, Justa shared her criticism:

I am uncomfortable because of the comment I made to Adrienne earlier: 'When you are older, Adrienne, you will understand.' I want to examine my own ageism because I am committed to creating a safe space here and think my remark was divisive and obstructive in contributing to that, not only for Adrienne, but for others as well.

At first, Adrienne did not respond. Two other women in the group tried to reassure Justa that her remark was not ageist. They thought the remark showed Justa's desire to "help" Adrienne. Others in the group, however, began to share their perceptions which confirmed the ageist implications of the remark.

After thoughtful reflection and hearing others' perceptions, Adrienne could tune in to her own sense. She shared with the group that she felt angry when she heard the remark, but her awareness at the time had only been partial. Her immediate re-·sponse had been to scold herself internally, and to rationalize that Justa was sincere and therefore she should not have those negative feelings. She acknowledged that without the group's focus, she would have left the gathering with a sense of distance from Justa, a sense of not belonging to the group, most of whom were older than herself, and discounting her own reality. She also reflected that she probably would not have realized exactly why. Now that the group had addressed it openly, she could acknowledge what had happened, and her reflections helped the group to examine the meaning of the instance. Once Adrienne focused the group's attention on *her* reality, everyone's awareness of ageism and its divisiveness increased immensely.

Criticism as Homework

Sometimes you cannot think clearly and speak artfully at the time of Closing. Often, people can only do so after the meeting is over. This gives you the opportunity to do your own internal work at home, especially when it comes to critical reflections. If you sense during a meeting that there is a criticism you need to develop at home, say during Closing the nature of your concern, and ask the group to wait for a fuller criticism at the next gathering, either during Check-In or as an agenda item.

Give criticism at a time when the group is receptive, open, and ready to address the concerns in your criticism. You may need to wait for a time that is right, or ask the group to plan for a time that can be set aside to address the issue.

Artful criticism arises from your deepest feelings, is energized by your emotions, and is finely crafted by your clearest thinking. It is shared with others in a manner and at a time when full awareness (including thoughts and feelings) can be called upon to address the issue. The homework required to do this includes getting in touch with the full range of feelings that you experience around the issue, and thinking about all of the facts and circumstances that are a part of the situation. It requires thinking through similar circumstances that you have experienced to search for a perspective that comes from that broader experience, and envisioning future possibilities that might emerge from this experience.

Constructive critical reflection is placed in the context of the purposes of the group. One way to do this is to take time to review the group's Principles of Unity. Think about the present situation in light of each principle and how addressing the issue you are studying can strengthen the group.

Weigh carefully many possibilities. Imagine what might be different in a similar circumstance in the future, as well as possibilities that may emerge from the situation as it is. Think about how you and the group might move forward in a direction that you carefully choose rather than a direction that just happens.

As you reflect on the situation, write ideas and thoughts on a sheet of paper. You can go over these notes to sort out which of your ideas are beneficial and constructive, and re-think ideas that may not be constructive. Once you see your ideas on paper, you can explore different ways of saying things, and make sure everything you need to say is there. When you share your ideas with the group, the notes you prepare at home can help you remain focused, and include your full range of feelings and thoughts, stated in constructive and beneficial ways.

Creating Affirmations

Affirmations often grow out of internal work that you do apart from the group, and your experiences in the group. This work involves shifting your attention away from frustrations and problems to possibilities for growth and change. As you reflect on these possibilities, you will begin to form affirmations that provide a message to your inner consciousness that you are receptive to the energy of change moving in a creative, healing direction.

Since the inner consciousness is responsive to repetition, repeat affirmations to yourself, using the same wording again and again (with shifts in the wording as you find what is most comfortable for you). Repeat the affirmations while you are doing rhythmic activities, such as exercising, cleaning, or walking. When you re-enter the group, you will bring with you the deep inner resources that you have developed within yourself to more effectively participate in the group.

These examples are affirmations you can use while you are becoming accustomed to using them:

- I value the light and clarity that I bring to situations.[7]
- All that I know is available to me when I need it.
- I believe in myself and our group.
- I care for my Self.
- I am at peace with those I love.
- I am in tune with my intuition.
- I believe in the power of our group.
- I act with confidence in my ability.
- The love we share for each other nourishes me.
- I willingly release the old and welcome the new in my life.
- I choose wisely because I listen to my inner voice.
- I gladly accept the support of those with whom I work.
- My love for my self brings love and support to all my relationships.

9

Valuing Diversity and Unity:
Conflict Transformation

Your group values diversity and unity if . . .

- You can name at least *one* thing your group does during every meeting that reflects the valuing of each individual.
- You can identify at least *two* recent occasions when your group's decisions considered the minority view.
- You can describe at least *three* Principles of Unity held in common by each member of your group.
- You can name at least *four* recent occasions when the leadership in your group shifted spontaneously in response to the issue under discussion.
- You can identify (in your group's most recent meeting) at least *five* instances when members freely expressed appreciation for one another.
- You can describe at least two points of disagreement that your group is currently considering;
- And, for each of the two points, you can describe at least three distinctly different perspectives that the group is considering.

Conflict transformation involves ways of knowing and doing that are central to *Peace and Power* processes. Conflict transformation draws especially on the powers of diversity and unity. The Power of Diversity means encouraging creativity, valuing alternative views, and encouraging flexibility. The Power of Unity means integrating variety within the group (see Chapter 2). Even at the best of times, enacting these powers is not always possible. When a group cannot integrate diversity or variety, the group inevitably becomes engaged in conflict. Typically groups deal with conflict by ignoring it, backing away from it, getting caught up in it, or "agreeing to disagree."

To move beyond the typical patterns of dealing with conflict, it is important to realize the subtle ways in which habits of "power-over powers" may creep into your group interactions, and to develop ways to use the PEACE powers of Diversity and Unity. Making this shift will involve learning to embrace conflict as an opportunity for growth and as an important part of group experience. Unity does not come from agreement or from "making nice." Rather, using open and conscious practices to address conflict are among the most important steps toward creating unity and toward valuing diversity in group interactions.

RE-DEFINING CONFLICT

Patriarchal definitions of the word "conflict" refer to incompatibility, opposing action, antagonism, and hostility.[1] Underlying those definitions is the suggestion of the potential for violence. Given how people learn language, all of the connotations of conflict are immediately known to us at some level—little wonder that conflict is something people often try to avoid.

In fact, conflict is *not* always the same thing as hostility, antagonism, or incompatibility. Differences of opinion, disagreements, argument—all forms of conflict that may not involve hostility or violence—happen in all groups. However, a simple disagreement can quickly escalate into something that carries feelings of antagonism, polarization of viewpoints into "right and wrong," and open hostility.

A number of approaches to dealing with conflict are very effective (conflict resolution, negotiation, arbitration), and the *Peace and Power* approaches to conflict transformation draw on many of these. Of necessity, many approaches focus on reducing hostilities and on an outcome of compromise between opposing groups or individuals. The best approaches seek "win-win" solutions.

Peace and Power approaches are designed to *transform* conflict itself. In conflict transformation, the group addresses the immediate issue in constructive ways, but attention shifts toward group learning. Everyone grows in understanding the group's values, and uses the conflict process to develop new skills that contribute to the group's unity and ability to integrate diversity.

A first step in moving toward a reality where conflict is valued and valuable is to recognize the limits of adversarial definitions of conflict, and to create a new way of thinking about conflict. In American English, there are no words to express the peaceful, even welcomed co-existence of differing points of view, different perspectives, or different ideas about how things are to be done. When people in the group have opinions about an issue that reflect disagreement in a *Peace and Power* process, honest discussion can happen without hostility, antagonism, or competition for being "right." Even when people have strong feelings, even hostility or antagonism, transforming conflict into something beneficial for the group and for individuals is possible. Being able to do this depends on knowing that you have a *choice* in dealing with conflict, and that you can learn ways to transform conflict, other than reducing or eliminating hostility and antagonism.

Conflict transformation is a process that involves:

- Practicing skills in everyday group interactions that build a foundation for addressing conflict when it happens.
- Learning individual ways of responding to conflict constructively.
- Recognizing and acknowledging conflict or potential for conflict early in an interaction.
- Making deliberate choices to address the conflict constructively.
- Enacting powers of diversity and unity in the group to encourage creativity and to integrate variety.

FOUNDATIONS FOR TRANSFORMING CONFLICT INTO UNITY AND DIVERSITY

Conflict transformation begins before there is conflict in a group. It is very difficult—often impossible—to transform conflict by waiting until conflict happens and *then* begin to work on ways to deal with it differently. Groups can do three important things during times of relative calm that build a strong foundation for transforming conflict. These are:

Nurturing a strong sense of rotating leadership within the group. A group that has practiced rotating leadership can turn to those who have the clarity, vision, and energy to address a conflict constructively when it happens (see Chapters 5 and 6). Effective leadership can re-focus the group's attention and provide clear guidance in staying focused on the underlying issues rather than simply getting lost in the immediate conflict itself. Refocusing is a critical element to bring about transformation; it places the conflict in a greater context so that people can respond to the greater implications and long-term effects of the conflict. If every individual within a group has experience at being a leader, each person already feels strong and supported in their leadership role, and can comfortably move into this role when the group experiences conflict.

Practicing constructive criticism. Critical reflection (see Chapter 8) provides a way to move out of communication styles of blaming, hostility, and damaging verbal assaults. Instead, members of the group develop skills of communication that focus on the group's responsibility for what happens in the group, and on future possibilities for constructive growth and change. Practice in using critical reflection when no conflict is involved builds the necessary skills in a safe context, and develops the group's confidence in critical reflection as a safe and welcomed process. Critical reflection practiced regularly develops clarity about the group's Principles of Unity so that when conflict occurs this clarity is a resource for addressing the conflict. If everyone has practiced and feels familiar with critical reflection, when conflict happens and someone begins using critical reflection in addressing the conflict, it brings a sense of safety and commitment to the process, rather than a sense of fear and dread.

82

Practicing ways to value diversity. If your group has established habits that draw you closer toward valuing individual differences, then when you do experience conflict you will have a strong basis from which to transform the conflict. Intense feelings typically narrow or restrict a member's ability to remain open. Habits of valuing diversity lay a foundation to be open to considering many options even when feelings are running high. The processes of Check-In (see Chapter 5), and Closing (see Chapter 8) are two ways for groups to habitually recognize, honor, and celebrate diversities that exist within the group. When conflict occurs, you already know and appreciate diverse perspectives, interests, and talents that individuals bring to the situation. In transforming conflict the group learns more about themselves but also builds on the foundation of diversity that they already appreciate.

INDIVIDUAL APPROACHES THAT TRANSFORM CONFLICT

Conflict within a group is a group responsibility; however, each individual can take significant steps toward changing patterns of behavior and communication that contribute to old patterns of dealing with conflict. You can practice three skills to change your personal habits of dealing with conflict:

- The gentle art of verbal self defense.
- Reclaiming the virtues of gossip, and
- Appreciating anger as a source of strength.

The Gentle Art of Verbal Self Defense

Suzette Haden Elgin has developed a system of language behavior that is simple to learn and that creates dramatic shifts in interaction patterns.[2] In *Staying Well with the Gentle Art of Verbal Self-Defense*,[3] she teaches readers specific skills to reduce hostility in human interactions, and in turn improve both individual and group well-being. Using the gentle art of verbal self defense makes

83

it possible to get out of negative loops of hostile verbal interactions and move instead into language that opens the way for greater understanding of differences.

Suzette describes twenty-one techniques. Four of her suggestions are particularly helpful in developing skills that are useful in group interactions. Two of these are already part of *Peace and Power* processes.

Applying Miller's Law: Miller's law states, "In order to understand what another person is saying, you must assume that it is true and try to imagine what it could be true of."[4] This does not mean that you always agree that what the person says is true, but you step into their perspective—and assume that this is true for them. Especially when you are aware that you are about to dismiss what someone has said because it is ridiculous, shift your thinking to apply Miller's law. Your response shifts to saying to the person—"I hear what you are saying. Tell me more about what you mean."

Avoiding hostile modes of communication: When you engage in hostile communication, you are not really dealing with an issue, and, you harm yourself and other people. Contrary to what many people believe, hostile communication does nothing to make anyone feel better (the old "get it off your chest" myth). Suzette's specific approaches for avoiding hostile communication are based on the awareness that "anything you feed will grow."[5] If someone attacks by blaming, for example, if you blame back or counterblame, the cycle of blaming will grow and grow. Instead, you can use a simple, factual unemotional statement in what Suzette calls "the computer mode." An example of a hostile, blaming statement is: "If you REALly CARED about this GROUP, you would keep your PROBlems to yourSELF." A response that feeds the hostility and blame is the familiar "WHO do you think YOU are to act as if YOU never bring YOUR problems to this GROUP." A response that would interrupt the loop would be "It is interesting to consider that people's problems influence group interaction." This is a "computer mode" response that does not blame anyone; it moves away from the hostility and sends the clear message "I am not going to participate in a negative interaction." Unlike more familiar responses of simply ignoring the blamer, or walking away from the situation, responses that effectively interrupt a negative or hostile verbal interaction also send the message "I will stay and talk, but I will not do so in a way that hurts."

Using three-part messages: When you are addressing a conflict or a potential conflict, Suzette suggests a message that has the components:

When you . . .
I feel . . .
Because . . .

These are like the components for a critical reflection.[6] You can practice the specific *Peace and Power* approaches to critical reflection (see Chapter 8) in your daily interactions with people. You can also refer to Suzette's excellent guidelines to learn and practice this type of communication.[7]

Syntonic listening.   *Peace and Power* processes require active listening, particularly during discussion when you are using Rotating Chair, when people are Checking-In or Closing, and when you are addressing conflict. Syntonic listening is like active listening, which is remaining fully engaged with the other person without letting your mind wander to another topic, or to your own responses to what the person is saying. Suzette suggests practicing the art of syntonic listening by listening to a boring speaker on television for at least ten minutes. Your challenge is to practice *not* letting your mind wander to other things. When you can "stay tuned" you will be better able to be aware of "tuning out" when it is important for you to be giving a speaker your full and undivided attention.

The gentle art of verbal self defense is accessible and possible to learn even in less than ideal circumstances. You can work with any of Elgin's books on your own, or you can work with others in your group to practice new language behaviors in your group. You will find that even one or two shifts in how you habitually respond to hostility will create dramatic changes in your verbal interactions, making it possible to experience conflict in ways that move away from the hostility and toward constructive ways of dealing with differences.

Reclaiming the Virtues of Gossip

Talk outside the group about people and events in the group, commonly known as gossip, can be a destructive source of group conflict or it can be an important source of group energy. Gossip is a skill linked with women's talk.[8] Gossip, like many other words in the English language that refer primarily to women, once had a positive meaning that has now been distorted to a negative meaning. Originally, the word "gossip" was a noun for the woman who assisted the midwife at the time of birth. The "gossip" was the labor coach, and after the birth she went into the community to spread the news about the birth. She was considered a very wise woman who could communicate the wisdom of the stars.[9]

Groups can reclaim the art of gossip[10] to develop new ways of talking about one another and events in the group. The talk shared among group members in the less structured setting outside the group can be an important source of energy that, like the labor coach, helps to give birth to the ideas and visions of the group. Constructive and energizing gossip builds on the values of *Peace and Power*. The ethics of gossip that follow assure talk that is constructive and growthful:

- Gossip is to be purposeful. When you tell a story about someone or something, tell why you are sharing the story. For example, if you are telling your friend about a budding sexual involvement between two members of the group, share that the reason you want to talk about it is because of your concern for the sensitivity of the situation in the group, and that you are seeking ways to interrupt the divisiveness that could result. When you and your friend both enter into gossip with this type of reason, you will move away from talk that derides, blames, or otherwise damages the people involved. Instead, your talk will focus on how the group can respond to the situation in ways that are respectful and that protect the integrity of the group. If you cannot name a reason to gossip that comes from a shared purpose, you should turn your talk to another topic.

- Own your Self. Focus on your own feelings and ideas, rather than what you think someone else felt or thought. Although

86

you may be concerned about how other people in the group may feel or react to an emerging sexual involvement between two people in the group, focus your gossip on how *you* feel about it, and what your thoughts are about how it may contribute to divisiveness in the group.

- Name your source. When passing along information, be clear about how you came by the information. Share who told you about what happened, or how you know about what happened. If you cannot name your source, then do not pass along the information. Do not say, for example, "the committee decided to deny your petition." If you were not there when the committee decided, say how you know about the decision: "Nancy, who chairs the committee, has told me that the committee denied your petition." If you were there, say: "I was present when the committee voted to deny your petition, and I was one of the people who voted to deny because . . ."

- Be cautious about presenting information in a way that could be used to hurt another person; give information in a way that opens possibilities for greater compassion and understanding. For example, information that could be hurtful would be to leave a class saying: "I was astonished at what Priscilla said in class today! She really is intolerant!" A message that could convey the same astonishment, but not misrepresent or label Priscilla, would be: "I was astonished when I heard Priscilla's views on the militarization of women's lives. I need to think through how to continue this discussion the next time we meet."

- Affirm the opportunity and possibility for growth and change. When talking about Priscilla's comments on militarization, examine various points that you think need to be explored to move the discussion toward constructive understanding. Gossip that focuses on what else needs to happen moves toward greater understanding of the issues.

- Use humor as a way to address emotions, and to shed light on a situation. Be very cautious about hurtful, diminishing teasing. Never knowingly tease or ridicule another person, and be cautious about humor that is self-denigrating. For example, suppose you are telling a story about being put down when you spoke up as a student in a committee meeting. A comment made with a laughing tone: "I guess I am just an unimportant student who has no business expressing my opinion" is not funny, nor is it dry humor. It is self-denigrating, and it passively implies ridicule of others about whose opinions you are only speculating. Instead, you could tell your story about how people responded to your speaking up as a student, and proclaim "Students arise!" to move toward an affirming, joyful statement that off-sets your distress with the negative response you received.

- Use information to share and inform, not to manipulate. For example, if you honestly think that your friend is doing something wrong, then provide *all* the information you can that might help enlighten the situation, without prodding or coercing your friend to decide in the direction you want. Refrain especially from making bold proclamations (which are always really speculations) about the future as a way to frighten the person to decide your way. Leave the decision to your friend, even if it may turn out to be one with which you do not agree.

- Use gossip to assist and to build community, not to compete. When you hear another person's story, stay away from responding with a "one-up" story of your own. Instead, focus on sharing ideas and feelings about what her story means to you, and how together you can learn from the story. For example, if a friend tells you about a terrible thing that has happened at work when they gave pay raises, do not launch into your own "ain't it awful" story about when your boss denied you a pay raise. Instead, say that you have had an experience that is similar, but keep the focus of the discussion on what your friend has experienced and is learning about the politics of her work life.

Anger As a Source of Strength

Anger is a feeling that many people, especially women, have learned to deny. Understandably, women have learned to fear the anger of others because it is so closely linked to life-threatening violence against women. Women's anger especially can elicit life-threatening violence, further enforcing fear of one's own anger. Like the word conflict, anger is a word used in many societies to

88

cover many negative feelings and dynamics in human relationships. While anger is a fundamental feeling, other feelings and dynamics acquire the label as well. Anger is not the same thing as hatred, dislike, repulsion or envy. Emotions like hatred, repulsion or envy are not sources of strength in the way that anger can be.

In groups committed to shifting ways of working with one another, dealing constructively with anger is a major step toward creating safety needed to deal with conflict. Steps you can practice to learn new ways to deal with anger as a source of strength are:

- Recognize that your anger (real anger, not hatred or envy) is a valuable tool or clue that something different needs to happen. Learn to take the time to move away from the situation until you are clear about what needs to happen differently. Use your anger as a signal that you need to step away from the situation until you think through exactly what needs to change.

- Rehearse safe ways to acknowledge your anger with people who can support your growth, and understand what you are working on. You can use critical reflection approaches in either role-plays you set up, or in relatively safe real-life situations. Rehearse when you are not feeling angry, but work with situations that have in the past, or could in the future, make you feel very angry. Rehearsing ways to acknowledge your anger will help you overcome your fear of anger, so that it no longer immobilizes you but becomes a source of strength.

- Realize that confrontation is usually not a constructive approach to dealing with anger. Instead, confrontation usually polarizes and distances you from other people involved in the situation. Once you take the time to get clear about the "signal" that your anger represents, then you can think through approaches that address the situation directly and calmly, moving toward constructive changes in the situation.[11] Practice using critical reflection in groups, giving special attention to how you share what you want to happen next. Notice how the group responds to your insights, and invite them to give you constructive suggestions.

GROUP APPROACHES TO TRANSFORMING CONFLICT

Whenever conflict enters the awareness of the group as a whole, or individuals within the context of the group, it is group conflict. It is always tempting to dismiss conflict as "personality differences," assuming that the two or three individuals will just have to work it out. While it is indeed desirable for individuals to resolve personal differences, conflict or hostile interactions within the group require a group response if it is to be transformative for the group.

Group conflict is no *one* person's responsibility; no one or two individuals can resolve group conflict even if they resolve a conflict between themselves. Group conflict is *everyone's* responsibility. The outcome of openly dealing with conflict is *transformation* where every individual learns, gains new insights, and experiences new possibilities. When conflict is addressed in a group, everyone learns from the many different points of view. Rather than having to resolve two points of view of individuals who are "at odds" in a group, several different people speak to the issue and many more possibilities emerge. The rich exchange that happens in this process brings forth many possibilities that exist among group members and provides insight from which awareness of common ground emerges.

Peace and Power processes offer three distinct group actions that bring about transformation of conflict. These are:

- Owning group conflict.
- Interrupting habits that sustain divisiveness.
- Finding unifying values and diverse possibilities.

Owning Group Conflict

When conflict occurs in a group, it is often initially expressed as if it were a conflict between two individuals, or between two opposing "factions" within the group. In reality, anything that happens in a group context belongs to the group—including those who may not be directly involved or invested in the issue at hand. If

90

you isolate opposing individuals or factions within the group by labeling it as simply "their issue," others in the group fail to recognize and own group dynamics that contribute to the situation—dynamics that everyone in the group shares.

To move toward group ownership of the conflict, everyone in the group participates in discussion that clarifies how the conflict relates to the group's purpose and principles of unity. The group seeks diverse points of view and possibilities for reaching new understandings. While claiming group ownership of a conflict, the group brings misunderstandings of the conflict to light, each individual sees the situation from the fresh perspective that comes from group wisdom, and real shifts in attitude and in action can begin to flow.

For example, Chullie, Justa, Lynn, Sue, and Betty formed a writers' support group and decided to meet weekly over the summer. Chullie and Justa were the most experienced writers in the group and the other women often turned to them for guidance. One of their Principles of Unity, however, was to equalize the balance of power among them through sharing information and through valuing each person's writing skills. Over several weeks, Justa became aware that whenever Lynn asked a question, it was directed only to Justa. When Justa spoke, Lynn paid careful attention and when others spoke Lynn appeared uninterested. When Lynn had the chair, she looked only at Justa and always managed to sit where she could maintain eye contact with Justa. Justa became very uncomfortable with what she perceived as "shero-worship." Justa was aware that she had not yet reached full understanding of exactly what it was that bothered her so much, but she decided that she needed to address the issue in the group before her irritation became so great she could not deal constructively. During Closing at the next gathering, Justa shared her critical reflection:

> "I am growing increasingly uncomfortable—near a point of anger—every time I notice that Lynn is only directing questions to me, or mostly looks at me, and does not pay attention when other people in the group talk. I am concerned because we have made a commitment to equalize power among us, and this interaction is

setting me up as an expert, at least where Lynn is concerned. I want everyone in the group to think about this and at our next gathering share your perceptions—which may not be like mine—so that we can discuss what is going on and how we can be sure we are changing the balance of power here."

At Check-In the following week, Betty responded to Justa's criticism by saying that she thought the issue between Lynn and Justa was a personality conflict and that Justa was overly sensitive about her status as a successful writer. Chullie said that she had observed, and resented Lynn's admiration of Justa to the exclusion of others, and suggested that the group needed to look at how each person was contributing to the interactions between Justa and Lynn. Sue did not speak to the issue during Check-In. Lynn began to cry and denied that she was treating Justa differently than she treated anyone else. After several exchanges that moved the group further into confusion and misunderstanding, they agreed to meet again later that week to look only at this issue and to place tasks "on hold" until they could resolve the conflict.

While their Principles of Unity reflected the ideal that members of this group were seeking better ways to work together and to equalize power imbalances, they encountered a conflict that could remain isolated as an issue between two people. If they dismissed it as an issue between two people, however, the issue would continue to plague the effective working relationships within the group. By the time of the meeting to discuss the conflict, Sue moved into a leadership role and prepared a SOPHIA that consciously re-focused the group's awareness on their Principles of Unity: "We will seek to equalize the balance of power among us." She placed the following subjective before the group: What are each of our perceptions of the situation now that we have thought it through? What possible new directions can we imagine to equalize our balance of power?

Chullie shared her perception that Justa often speaks eloquently to the topic of discussion, but does not facilitate other people expressing their point of view. In fact, Chullie observed, Justa's ability to be so articulate sometimes felt very intimidating. Betty, who had not noticed any of these dynamics, shared that the open expression of the conflict had given her the awareness that she had continued to feel like a real novice in the group and that this feeling, she now realizes, was keeping her relatively unempowered as a writer. Lynn, who sincerely had not intended to treat Justa differently, began to realize that she had a habit of deferring to people she respects highly, and that her deference unconsciously sustained a power dynamic that she indeed found distasteful, but did not know how to interrupt. Additionally, she realized that she had not noticed the particular skills that Sue and Chullie also brought to the group, and had assumed that Betty was there, like herself, merely to learn how to write from the one person she recognized as an expert.

Once the group had entered into a full discussion of their perspectives, several things happened. Lynn consciously interrupted her doting behavior and asked the group's feedback and support for acting on her intention to sustain mutually respectful relationships with everyone in the group. Justa realized that she felt a certain "performance anxiety" to always provide answers and was relieved to be able to relax and interact without having to be the teacher. She had not been aware that her ready answers were interfering with others' ability to contribute. Justa shared her intention to honor other women's contributions before assuming she had the answers. She began working with the affirmation "I value the talents of everyone in the group." Betty gained a new appreciation for a talent she had not previously realized that she had in proofreading and accurate spelling. She made a commitment to the group to bring these skills to the group. Everyone laughed when Justa acknowledged that she (Justa) is a terrible speller and proofreader, something the group had not realized. Sue and Chullie reflected on their experiences of taking risks and assuming the responsibility of voicing difficult insights about particular situations. Sue had said some brave things during her SOPHIA, and appreciated the group's responses. Chullie had confronted the effects of Justa's actions, which had been very difficult for her because she feared that Justa might misunderstand. Sue and Chullie gained a new respect for their own leadership skills and ability to stay with an uncomfortable situation until it was throughly explored.

In this example, the key to transforming the conflict was to own the conflict as a group problem. If the group had continued to isolate the problem as existing between Justa and Lynn, nothing new could have happened; in fact the same old patterns of hurt feelings, continued aggravation, and frustration would have persisted. In first owning, and then transforming the conflict, each individual gained new insights about her unique strengths; each individual also gained self-knowledge of ways she could change and grow. This group truly moved toward honoring diversity within the group, while at the same time growing in awareness of unifying values upon which their diversity rested.

Interrupting Habits that Sustain Divisiveness

Divisiveness is an all-too familiar experience among groups. Divisiveness obscures commonalities, side-tracking groups from developing unity and diversity. Most of the things that sustain divisiveness in groups are habits that people have learned as the "right," "assertive," "savvy," or "political" way to deal with group interactions. In fact, these habits are rooted in power-over values where the individual is assumed to be at odds with the group and with other individuals in the group. Integrating differences is not conceived as a possibility, much less a value. This list shows examples of what happens when you are nurturing diversity, contrasted with what happens when you are engaged in divisiveness.[12]

Diversity	*Divisiveness*
When I am convinced that my point of view is the only reasonable one:	
I still take the time to find out what other people think.	I keep repeating it to make sure that everyone hears it.

Valuing Diversity and Unity: Conflict Transformation

Diversity	*Divisiveness*

When things become tense in a discussion, and "sides are being drawn":

I encourage discussion so that each point of view is fully presented.	I usually know what side I am on and grow impatient with drawn out discussions.

In a meeting:

I make sure I express my point of view and limit my comments so that others may also speak to the issue.	I make sure I express my point of view at length so that others don't miss out on all the implications of my insights.

When I am aware that something I have said or done has bothered others:

I stop to consider what has happened and try to put myself in their shoes.	I figure it is their problem and it is up to them to work it out.

When others are expressing their views:

I actively listen and hear them out before framing my response.	I usually already know what they are trying to say and jump in to say what I have to say to move the discussion along.

When there is disagreement in the group:

I invite everyone to express their viewpoints so that we can all hear, and consider these in reaching a decision.	I think the best way to deal with it is simply to agree to disagree, and not get caught up in trivia.

When I am unable to attend a scheduled meeting:

I make sure someone knows my concerns about relevant issues and is willing to take them to the group.	I figure I can catch up at the next meeting and let people know what I think.

Establishing Unifying Values and Diverse Possibilities

A key to conflict transformation is determining the value (or values) that bring the group together, and then identifying the unifying value from which the conflict emerges. This is not easy to do. Often, the group names the conflict itself in such a way that the unifying value is obscured, but in all group conflict there is at least one unifying value. When conflict occurs, something about the conflict matters to the members of the group in a significant way. If the issue did not matter, there would be no conflict. The value may not be a value the group is seeking to enact—it could even be a value they are seeking to overcome. The process of figuring out the unifying value underlying the conflict, or why it matters so much to the members of the group, always helps to clarify what values the group chooses. With the unifying value or values clarified, the members of the group can explore diverse possibilities for addressing the conflict itself.

As an example, a conflict that is common among feminist groups involves different perspectives on the question: "What is feminism?" No group will ever answer this type of question to everyone's satisfaction, and often members of a group grow weary of the debate. Discussions that focus on trying to find an answer leads to divisiveness, polarizations, and judgmental attitudes toward one another for not being "politically correct." Instead, a group can turn attention to identifying what unifying value is motivating their continued discussion on this issue. This type of conflict often is rooted in deep feelings and individual values about "who am I and who should we be together?" If the group moves to a discussion about who they want to be together, they are likely to arrive at a concrete expression that in fact also defines feminism for the group. For example they might agree to be "strong women who value and respect the experience of all women." With this statement, they can now discuss how various definitions of feminism fit with who they want to be, and embrace a wide range of possibilities. If they agree to be "people who actively seek to overcome all forms of injustice in the world," their discussion of various definitions of feminism will be somewhat different, but they will still be able to embrace a wide range of definitions of feminism. By making this "move" to establish their unifying values and diverse possibilities, the group steps away from discussions of individual (sometimes competing) preferences, abstract ideas, or individual beliefs, and toward the collective, concrete purpose that brings them together.

In work groups or classrooms, if the group spends time building consensus around a specific value they want to enact to guide their work, (see Chapter 3 or 11 for suggestions), then they may also explore the wide diversity of perspectives that they bring to being able to act on this value. For example, a work group began experiencing conflict when Linda started bringing to the group's awareness the financial bind that the group was in. Over several months members of the group expressed anger and resentment at Linda for being so picky, and at one another for either doing or not doing something to create the gloomy financial picture. When the group explored their unifying value, they realized that they all cared deeply about keeping the project going. They realized that to keep the project going, they needed to acknowledge and value what Linda was telling them, and what she could teach them about their finances. They agreed that they all wanted to focus their energy on creating financial stability to sustain the project. Linda, who had been taking the brunt of much of the group's resentment, began to relax. Her sharp wit and sense of humor began to return so that when she presented information to the group, she could do so in ways that invited them to be open. As the group began to explore the various approaches that they each thought the group should take in dealing with the problem, they became aware of many creative and useful ideas that already existed in the group—ideas about solutions that had been obscured by the group's focus on blame and judgment about the "cause" of the problem. Several solutions implied ways they could prevent the situation from happening again in the future—approaches that Linda, and others responsible for the finances of the group had not thought about. The most important transformation that occurred was a shift in how they interacted when dealing with difficult issues.

WHEN TRANSFORMATION OF CONFLICT IS NOT POSSIBLE

Sometimes transforming conflict is not possible. It is well worth the effort to work toward the ideal for some time before giving up. Often, when it seems impossible, real movement toward the ideal *is* possible. When you and the group finally recognize that you cannot transform a conflict in an ideal sense, turn your energy to exploring what *is* possible to create better working relationships. In groups where membership is voluntary, it may be that it is time consider ending the group altogether (see Chapter 10). Some voluntary groups, and groups that are obligated to continue to work together might seek outside assistance in creating better working relationships. Even when less than ideal circumstances are the best that you can do, you can carry with you insights that come from the experience, and build from the experience in the future.

10

Period Pieces

Things happen in every group periodically, but not at every gathering. Some of these happenings are pleasant and welcome. Others are less pleasant and are unwelcome. *Peace and Power* processes call for an awareness and anticipation of periodic group issues and challenges. Groups that last over time develop practices and rituals related to their predictable periodic happenings.

PERIODIC REVIEW OF PRINCIPLES OF UNITY

Periodically reviewing Principles of Unity is like cleaning house. It is something groups often delay or neglect. Nevertheless, it is necessary for group well-being and feels good once it is done! Some groups select a season of the year as a time for looking over what is being done, and thinking about changes that the group needs to make. In other groups, the time for taking a new look at the old Principles comes when the focus shifts, such as when a task is completed, or when group membership changes.

Questions that are helpful in taking a critical look at principles of unity are:

- Are we actually *Doing* what this principle implies?
- If not, what *are* we doing?
- What *Principle* is implied in what we *are* doing?

99

In the Friendship Collective, for example, we began with a principle that we would expect no financial contribution from any member in relation to our work. In practice, we encountered expenses for each person who remained a part of the group. For some women these expenses were a problem. The review of our Principles of Unity made it possible to address these concerns, and find a way to state a principle that brought the tension of unrealistic financial pressures into the open.

OPEN OR CLOSED GROUPS?

In the ideal, *Peace and Power* groups usually seek to be open to all who wish to join. However, this is a decision that needs to be carefully considered. The work of the group and the purpose for which the group exists may not lend itself to being completely open. The dilemma becomes, then, how to remain open to new thoughts, to integrating diversity within the group, and yet remain effective in your work.

One way to address this dilemma is to think of openness as relative and changing rather than as an opposing choice of open or closed. Task-oriented groups often need to maintain stability in membership to meet the pressing demands of tasks that form their central purpose for gathering. As the demands of the tasks change, a natural flow of movement occurs as some people leave the group (sometimes temporarily), and others join. Groups that are essentially permanent, such as a group that operates a community shelter, can identify times when membership is open and develop traditions to educate and orient new members.

PEOPLE JOINING AN ONGOING GROUP

Integrating new members is a welcome, but difficult transition. In open groups, the demands of constantly integrating new members is a challenge that requires far more time and energy than the group typically expects. Since *Peace and Power* groups do not "work" like typical groups, people who are new to the group are essentially in new territory, in the midst of a culture that may be totally unfamiliar. The words spoken may be their language, but meanings of words take on a new character that existing members learn to take for granted. People who have not heard the language of *Peace and Power* often find themselves in a muddle trying to figure out what is really going on. Once a group is committed to welcoming new members, existing members need to be constantly aware of these dynamics, and establish ways to ease the transition. Time at each gathering needs to be set aside to explain and clarify what is going on.

Groups that require relative stability in membership may set aside times during the year when the orientation of new members is the only focus for gathering. The group carefully plans these events, with each member of the existing group taking responsibility for part of the orientation. A typical new member agenda includes a brief oral history of the group, a review of the principles of unity, an orientation to what the group does, and a description of the contributions expected of all members.

For example, in the Emma Book Store Collective, we planned new member potlucks four times a year, when those who were interested in joining the Collective could gather with us to learn about our history and our Principles of Unity, and to consider what was involved in membership. We expected everyone to staff the store four hours a week, and to gradually assume other tasks such as ordering new stock, managing the finances, planning for special occasions, working with other groups in the community, and taking care of the physical space. In the three months following a potluck, we expected new members to participate in each of the major activities of the business with an experienced collective member to become oriented to the tasks. In this way, each person had the opportunity to carefully consider making a lasting commitment.

MEMBER LEAVING A GROUP

In groups with unrestricted openness to membership, leaving the group may be a simple matter of not continuing to contribute financially, or dropping out of the gatherings. In groups that exist for a purpose that involves personal development, such as a reading group or a support group, the group's purpose may lead to a "live and let live" response to someone leaving.

However, a member leaving the group often creates a void in the group, and people want to acknowledge the leave-taking openly in some way. In a group where an individual's leaving has any consequences for the members of the group, it is especially important to state in the Principles of Unity what the group wants to happen when someone leaves. Creating traditions around this event, similar to the traditions of welcoming new members, is helpful in making this a smooth transition for the group and for the member who is leaving. Since this event represents both an ending and a new beginning, one way to approach it is similar to Closing, with an entire gathering devoted to a Closing concerning the leaving of the individual. Each group member takes the time to express appreciation, critical reflections, and affirmation which enable the person leaving, and everyone in the group, to carry new insights into their separate futures.

ASKING A MEMBER TO LEAVE A GROUP

As difficult as it may be, sometimes the energies of the group and of an individual are not harmonious with one another. Whatever the issue is, a group working with *Peace and Power* values will address it in some constructive way. The assumption that we can "live together happily ever after" is a mythical belief that simply is not consistent with reality. Ending one phase and beginning a new phase is not necessarily a failure. Still, it is very traumatic for everyone involved to acknowledge difficulty that leads to asking a member to leave.

When a group finds that one member is not able to function effectively as a group member, the issues must first be addressed openly, bringing to the discussion the fullest of intentions to act in a way that is consistent with the group's principles. The group explores all possible avenues for resolving the issues. The discussion continues until every member is certain that the avenue chosen is one that is good for the group as well as loving and protective for the individual.

ENDING A GROUP

Ending a group does not mean that the group has been a failure. Often it celebrates the completion of the purpose for which the group formed. If the purpose was not a specific task that the group can wrap up in a neat package, then knowing when the purpose has been accomplished may not be easily recognizable. For example, a group formed to provide support for one another may find that after a while, people have sources of support elsewhere that had not existed when the group was first formed. When this happens, the group may have evolved into something that is no longer meaningful. When coming to the group's gatherings begins to be more of a chore than a pleasure, it is time to consider ending the group.

Rather than let a group simply fizzle out, plan a specific event around which the group acknowledges their ending. The event provides a means for everyone to close this phase of their experience, taking something from it into the future. Planning a gathering for a final Closing of the group can be a rich and growthful experience.

11

Classrooms, Committees, and Institutional Constraints

Learning and teaching can take place in the interests of human liberation, even within institutions created for social control.

—Kathleen Weiler[1]

When you bring Peace and Power into a group that exists within hierarchical institutions, you bring a powerful influence toward transformation. You can use the methods of *Peace and Power* as a whole, or adapt them, or use them in part for moving to new power relations in traditional groups. Using the approaches of *Peace and Power* in existing institutions depends on the group making a conscious commitment to a value that they freely choose.

People enter traditional groups such as classrooms, work teams or committees expecting that the group will function as usual. When a different way of working together is presented, it is necessary to explain the reasons for making the shift. If the reasons clearly relate to what the group has already been seeking, then the transition is relatively easy. The group can consider *Peace and Power* approaches as a way to help achieve their desired objectives.

Classrooms are especially well-steeped in traditions and constrained by institutional rules. *Peace and Power* approaches can be a breath of fresh air in such settings, but they can also confuse people when it is not clear why the shift is happening. The traditional teacher-student power imbalance is familiar to everyone who has attended school, and everyone knows what to expect. The teacher has the power to grade, to offer opinions and judgments, and to speak. The institution defines the student as a receiver of grades, a receiver of the teacher's opinions and judgments, and the listener. Overcoming these expectations for roles and behaviors is not easy, and some institutional expectations cannot be ignored (such as the recording of grades to represent the achievement of a certain curricular or institutional standard).

Two values consistently welcomed by classroom participants are empowerment for all and demystification of content and processes (especially processes for grades). Although people might assume that these values are central to what education is all about, they are ironically consistently undermined in most classroom situations. When a teacher brings alternatives to the classroom that clearly enact the values of empowerment and demystification, dramatic change occurs in how "teaching" is done.

While the values of empowerment and demystification seem easy to embrace, the actual process of making the shift is a big challenge for everyone. Some people welcome the change, others respond with varying degrees of reserve, and others object at the outset. If people who object have no alternatives, it may not be possible to make the shift. When individuals who object have a choice (for example they can enroll in another section of a college course), they are free to leave the group and pursue an alternative. Individuals who are initially hesitant, but willing to stay with the group, frequently relate moving stories about the inner transformations that occur for them during the group's gatherings.[2]

Whoever introduces *Peace and Power* to the group may find it helpful to prepare some written or verbal orientation that is specific to the work of the group. Focus on both the *value* shift and the *process* shift that you are proposing. In classroom situations, the teacher can prepare a course syllabus in a way that makes the values explicit and reflects how the process will bring those values to life. A member of a work team can prepare a similar description for the group to consider.

The ways in which the ideas of *Peace and Power* influence the work of groups in hierarchical institutions will differ greatly from group to group. The value the group decides to adopt as their principle guides their choice of method. For example, if in a classroom the group decides to work with the value of "sharing" as a focus for their time together, there are many ways this can be done. They can share leadership through the rotating role of the Convener, and share participation by using Rotating Chair during discussions. The group may choose a traditional lecture format for some classes as an avenue for enacting the value of sharing by the teacher to overcome knowledge imbalances. Or, they can choose to have the teacher lecture for part of the class time, with Rotating-Chair style of discussion for another part of the time. In addition the group members can share drafts of their written work with one another as a way to exchange ideas freely. The possibilities are unlimited.

The key element in making decisions about *what* to do and *how* is clarity about what value the group chooses to embrace. From there, the diversity of ways to enact the value can flow from the group. The group can then periodically examine how well they are doing in creating the value and process changes they are seeking together.

Groups in institutions can handle the transition best if they choose one PEACE power as a starting point. Many groups work within traditions that alienate and divide individuals from one another and groups are often eager to find a different ideal to work toward. Choosing one PEACE power implies a unifying value, provides a focus for the shifts in interaction, and maintains a grounding for times when the confusion of change becomes overwhelming.

The PEACE powers in Chapter 2, and the commitments in Chapter 3 are the basis for the suggestions in the following sections. Here the suggestions take into account typical challenges that you will encounter when you bring *Peace and Power* into an existing hierarchical institution. Some suggestions focus on individual behaviors, but all reflect fundamental shifts of value and attitude embraced by the whole group.

Power of Process:

Required structures such as objectives, time-frames or evaluation procedures are used as tools that provide a structure from which to work, but they are not the focal point. The *process* is the important dimension, so that the structure is *only* a tool and nothing more. *How* the interactions happen as you use the structure becomes the central focus, rather than a precise adherence to a prescribed procedure. Language is used as a tool to make the process possible, to create mental images that reduce the power imbalances defined by the institution, and to create new relationships. The process itself becomes an important focus for discussion along with the "content" in a classroom, or the "business" of the work group. Priorities related to decision-making shift, so that the urgency of making decisions lessens and the group learns to value wisdom that comes with the process. When this value is primary, Closing can be a powerful tool to learning to enact this value.

Power of Letting Go:

All participants let go of old habits and ways to make room for personal and collective growth. Teachers and work group chairs let go of "power over" attitudes and ways of being; class participants and work group members let go of "tell me what to do" attitudes and ways of being. Those who tend to dominate a discussion let go of their tendency to speak. Those who tend to remain silent let go of their tendency to sit back and watch. All participants move into ways of being that are personally empowering and that also nurture the empowerment of others. All participants share their ideas, but shift to a focus of fully hearing and understanding others' points of view.

Power of the Whole:

Mutual help networks within the group are encouraged. Old competitive habits are replaced with actions that reflect cooperation.

Each individual makes sure that everyone in the group has any and all information that is required to be successful. Every individual is responsible for using their talents and skills to address the interests of the group as a whole. Each participant, whether teacher or student, leader or member, is accountable to the *whole group* for negotiating specific agendas; keeping the group informed about absences, leaving early, arriving late; or initiating activities.

Power of Collectivity:

Each participant is taken into account in the group's planning-in-process. The group works to address the needs of those who are moving into individual journeys where others may not be going. The group in some way addresses the needs of those who are having specific struggles. Individuals do not compete with one another. Instead, the group acknowledges and addresses everyone's needs as equally valuable. The group takes into account every point of view within the group in making decisions.

Power of Unity:

The group recognizes Unity as coming from the expression of differing points of view so that all can understand, and integrate them into a richer and fuller appreciation of every individual. Out of this appreciation, each individual participates in clarifying the principle(s) that the group chooses to embrace. By actively seeking to understand differing perspectives that each person brings, the group can more fully understand what unifies them.

Power of Sharing:

All participants bring talents, skills, and abilities related to the work of the group, and actively engage in sharing their talents. Leaders and teachers enter groups with previously developed capabilities that are shared according to the needs of the group and in

109

consideration of the structure-as-tool. Members and participants enter the group with personal talents, background, and experiences that everyone values and shares. All participants enter the group open to what others can share, open to learning from every other member.

Power of Integration:

The group acknowledges all dimensions of the situation in planning their work. Each individual's unique and self-defined needs are acknowledged and integrated into the process. Everyone, not just the leader, participates in shaping how the group's work is done. The first portion of each gathering is set aside as a time for everyone to express their priorities, needs, and wishes for the gathering so that the group can integrate these as a part of the process for that gathering.

Power of Nurturing:

The group respects each participant fully and unconditionally, and regards every person as necessary and integral to the experience of the group. The group plans tasks, activities and approaches to nurture the gradual growth of new skills and abilities, assuring that *every* participant can be successful in reaching the goals of the group, and in meeting individual needs.

Power of Distribution:

Resources required for the work of the group (information, books, funds, space, transportation, equipment) are equally available and accessible to all members of the group. People share resources that individual members might purchase, such as books, equipment, or transportation (for example through libraries, laboratories, resource rooms or sharing among members), so that any individual who chooses not to use personal resources in this way, or who cannot, has equal access to the material. The group addresses issues arising from material inequalities among members openly to expose and overcome power imbalances perpetuated by economic privilege and disadvantage.

Power of Intuition:

The process that occurs, and the nature of what is addressed in the group, depend as much on the experience of the moment as on any other factor. What emerges as important for the group to address in the moment is what happens. The group lets go of what "ought" to happen to make possible what *will* happen. When institutional time-lines or performance expectations have to be a priority, the group acknowledges other things—what seems to be emerging as important for the group, and what the institution defines as important. The group then weighs which priority comes first, and how they can still address both priorities.

Power of Consciousness:

The group values ethical dimensions of the process as fundamental to the goals and purposes assigned to the group by the institution. The group considers every decision in terms of its ethical dimensions. Part of each gathering is devoted to a Closing—Appreciation, Critical Reflection, and Affirmation—as a way to move to group awareness of the values represented in what is done, and determine if these are the values the group intends.

Power of Diversity:

The group plans and enacts deliberate processes to integrate points of view of individuals and groups whose perspectives they do not usually address. The group deliberately includes experiences (through writings, personal encounters, poetry, song, drama, and more) of groups of different classes, of different countries, of women. Rotating Chair is one way to assure that everyone hears every voice in a group, so that the diversity that exists within the group can be expressed.

Power of Responsibility:

All participants assume full responsibility as the agent for their role in the process. Rotating Conveners is one way to nurture leadership. Rotating Chair assures that everyone has a way to assume responsibility for what happens in group meetings. Each individual assumes responsibility to demystify the processes involved in all activities, so that each member of the group has equal access to participating and understanding what is going on. In classrooms, "grades" become each individual's responsibility. Everyone shifts focus to what they are learning and accomplishing. The teacher or work group leader has a special responsibility to help demystify the workings of the institution, and to make explicit the political process within the institution.

Taking steps to adapt *Peace and Power* processes in hierarchical institutions can be risky, frightening, and discouraging. Sometimes your efforts will fail, and sometimes groups seem unable to move beyond mere token acts of working in ways that they envision. Often the hoped-for benefits and changes that happen seem completely invisible, only to become visible long after the group has ended. An important step that can be taken to overcome the isolation, fear, and frustration is to create a group outside the institution where *Peace and Power* values can be enacted more fully. This is usually a voluntary group committed to working together in order to create personal and social change. Experiencing a community, though it may be a small group, where the ideals may be realized more fully provides a place of centering, of concentrating energies in a healing direction, of support for the values that you are seeking to enact, and for exploring all that might be possible. Then, when the disappointments of the old world come crashing in, the visions of the new possibilities are there, somewhere.

Notes

Acknowledgments

1. Margaretdaughters, Inc. was created in 1984 by Charlene Eldridge Wheeler and Peggy L. Chinn. The name was a tribute to our Mothers, Margaret Eldridge and Margaret Tatum, who taught us the importance of "Doing what we Know." We published feminist writing, calendars and provided workshops on the use of *Peace and Power* until 1989 when we ended our publishing adventure, joining a large and respectable number of other small feminist presses that also succumbed to the realities of the publishing world.

2. Sue's dissertation is titled: *No More Fears: Peers Talk to Peers. An Activist Approach to Primary Care.* See also her article "The politics of caring: The role of activism in primary care," in *Advances in Nursing Science*, June, 1995, Vol. 17, No. 4, pp. 1–11.

3. Women war victims in Bosnia are currently using *Peace and Power* in their work with Merle Lefkoff.

Prologue

1. This quote is from a collection edited by Helen Forsey titled *Circles of Strength: Community Alternatives to Alienation,* Philadelphia: New Society Publishers, 1993, p. 1. This is an inspiring collection of stories of intentional communities, activist communities, religious or

spiritual communities—all groups of people forming different ways of living and working together.

2. Also from Forsey's collection, p. 2.

3. From the Foreword to Helen Forsey's collection in the first note, p. xii.

4. The links that I describe between *Peace and Power* processes and that which is feminist, are informed by the work of Elizabeth Frazer and Nicola Lacey in, *The Politics of Community: A Feminist Critique of the Liberal-Communitarian Debate.* (Toronto: The University of Toronto Press, 1993).

5. See Elise Boulding, *Building a Global Civic Culture: Education for an Interdependent World* (New York: Teachers College, 1988). In her chapter titled "Conflict, Diversity, and Species Identity," she addresses the two cultures of women and men and describes the work that women have done through women's culture to sustain society (pp. 62–64).

6. Mary Daly uses hyphens like this to convey a new possibility within the word, in this case meaning putting back together the pieces, the 'members', of what we Know as women. Her books *Gyn/Ecology* and the *Wickedary* provide enlightening study on her work with language and word usage (see the Notes in Chapter 2 for full references to Mary Daly's books).

7. Diane Stein, *All Women Are Healers: A Comprehensive Guide to Natural Healing* (Freedom, CA: The Crossing Press, 1980.) While this book is primarily an exploration of the various paths to natural healing, Diane looks at women's roles and contributions to healing. She weaves throughout her writing rich historical evidence, combined with well informed speculation about the origins of healing as women's art. For a detailed history of women as healers, see Jeanne Achterberg's book *Woman as Healer* (Shambhala Publications, Boston, 1991).

8. One of the most important books of this wave of feminism addresses the consistent and persistent erasure of women's knowledge and women's writing. In *Women of Ideas and What Men Have Done To Them* (Boston: Routledge & Kegan Paul, 1982), Dale Spender analyzes over three centuries of women's writing. She concludes: "We are women producing knowledge which is often different from that produced by men, in a society controlled by men. If they like what we produce they will appropriate it, if they can use what we produce (even against us) they will take it, if they do not want to know, they will lose it. But rarely, if ever, will they treat it as they treat their own" (p. 9). For several years,

this book was out of print and very difficult to find—a grim reminder of the enduring reality of Dale's insights. Most fortunately, this title has been re-released by Pandora Press, 1988, and remains in print.

9. These questions were inspired by a discussion of group conditions that support consensus presented in *Building United Judgment: A Handbook for Consensus Decision-Making* by Michel Avery, Brian Auvine, Barbara Streibel, and Lonnie Weiss. This is an excellent detailed resource if your group is making weighty decisions by consensus. It is published by the Center for Conflict Resolution, 731 State Street, Madison, WI 53703. Their phone number is (608) 255–0479.

10. Many people shared their thoughts about the creation of a Do-able peace list, sometimes not aware that their conversation was influencing our thinking. We were particularly influenced by the words and wisdom of: Connie Blair, Lorraine Guyette and other doctoral students (University of Colorado, School of Nursing, Spring 1991), Pat Hickson, Janet Quinn, Carole Schroeder and her children Ben and Morgan, Kelleth Chinn, and Christine Tanner.

Chapter One

1. Francis Moore Lappé, *Diet for a Small Planet: Tenth Anniversary Edition*. (New York: Ballantine Books, 1990), p. 15.

2. Anne Cameron, *Daughters of Copper Woman*. (Press Gang Publishers, 603 Powell Street, Vancouver, British Columbia, 1981), p. 53. Through the ancient myths of the native women of Vancouver Island, Anne Cameron offers "a shining vision of womanhood, of how the spiritual and social power of women—though relentlessly challenged—can Endure and Survive." (From the back cover). In the Preface, Cameron states: "From these few women, (the native women of Vancouver Island who told her the stories) with the help of a collective of women, to all other women, with love, and in Sisterhood, this leap of faith that the mistakes and abuse of the past need not continue. There is a better way of doing things. Some of us remember that better way."

3. Anne Cameron, as in the previous note, p. 63.

4. Elise Boulding, *Building a Global Civic Culture: Education for an Interdependent World*. (Teachers College Press, New York, 1988), p. 158.

5. Barbara Walker has contributed a major work that examines women's ancient wisdom and the past roles of female elders. She draws on carefully researched historical material to bring her clearly focused insights to current events and circumstances. See particularly *The Crone* (San Francisco: Harper and Row, 1985), *The Woman's Encyclopedia of Myths and Secrets* (New York: Harper and Row, 1983), and *The Skeptical Feminist: Discovering the Virgin, Mother and Crone* (San Francisco: Harper and Row, 1987).

6. Charlene and I adapted this definition of "praxis" from *Pedagogy of the Oppressed* by Paulo Friere, New York: The Seabury Press, 1970, p. 36. Our adapted definition emphasizes the synchronicity of thought and action.

7. In *A Passion for Friends: Toward a Philosophy of Female Affection* (Boston: Beacon Press, 1986), Janice Raymond provides a landmark vision of Gyn/affection, the ability to be moved by, and to deeply move other women. This profound experience of female friendship, formed in the cultural commitments that women make to their Selves and each other, is the grounding for women's personal and political empowerment.

8. A comprehensive exploration of a feminist concept of "empowerment" is in the premier issue of *Woman of Power: A Magazine of Feminism, Spirituality, and Politics,* Spring 1984. The journal is published quarterly by Woman of Power, Inc., P.O. Box 827, Cambridge, MA 02238.

9. Awareness is a central theme of feminist literature. In *The Politics of Reality: Essays in Feminist Theory* (The Crossing Press, 1983), Marilyn Frye explores a wide range of fundamental issues including oppression, sexism, and racism. In her essay titled "Lesbian Feminism and the Gay Rights Movement: Another View of Male Supremacy, Another Separatism," she states: "One of the privileges of being normal and ordinary is a certain unconsciousness. When one is that which is taken as the norm in one's social environment, one does not have to think about it . . . if one is marginal, one does not have the privilege of not noticing what one is. This absence of privilege is a presence of knowledge" (page 146).

10. A classic collection of feminist writings from the women's movement of the late 1960s and early 1970s is available in *Radical Feminism*, edited by Anne Koedt, Ellen Levine and Anita Rapone (New York: Quadrangle, 1973). In the essay "The Tyranny of Structurelessness" Joreen examines the informal elite patterns of decision-making that

exist in structured and unstructured groups, and the essential elements of "democratic structuring" necessary to achieve healthy functioning within a group. These elements include: delegation by the group, responsibility to the group, distribution of authority, rotation of tasks along rational criteria, diffusion of information, and equal access to resources. Our concept of consensus builds on and expands these concepts.

11. In *Pure Lust: Elemental Feminist Philosophy* (Boston: Beacon Press, 1984), Mary Daly states: "Although friendship is not possible among all feminists, the work of Be-Friending can be shared by all, and all can benefit from the Metamorphospheric activity. Be-Friending involves Weaving a context in which women can Realize our Self-Transforming, metapatterning participation in Be-ing. Therefore it implies the creation of an atmosphere in which women are enabled to be friends. Every woman who contributes to the creation of this atmosphere functions as a catalyst for the evolution of other women and for the forming and unfolding of genuine friendships" (p. 374).

Chapter Two

1. Notes from an interview on "Womanpower" with Joanna Rogers Macy in *Woman of Power,* Spring, 1984, page 12. Joanna Rogers Macy is co-founder of Interhelp (P.O. Box 331, Northampton, MA 01060), an international organization that provides workshops on "Despair and Empowerment in the Nuclear Age." Bobbi Levi, who leads these workshops in Massachusetts, provided this interview for *Woman of Power.*

2. Notes from an interview on "Womanpower" with Diane Mariechild in *Woman of Power,* Spring, 1984, page 18. Diane Mariechild is a mother, teacher, healer and author of *Motherwit: A Feminist Guide to Psychic Development* (Freedom, CA: The Crossing Press, 1981).

3. Grace Rowan, "Looking for a New Model of Power." *Woman of Power,* Spring, 1984, p. 67. She is described in this issue as "the co-founder of a shelter for battered women. She sees herself as a woman with power, and uses this power in her practice as a psychologist and for healing. She is a wise old woman on a journey to wholeness."

4. In this chapter I continue to capitalize and cast in bold the letters of the word PEACE to emphasize this word as representing Praxis, Empowerment, Awareness, Consensus, and Evolvement—the intentions and processes required for creating community.

5. Charlene and I first published a model of patriarchal power and feminist alternatives in *Cassandra: Radical Feminist Nurses News Journal*, Vol. 2, #2, May 1984, p. 10. This model is essentially the same model, but I have changed the "labels" to more clearly reflect what each tradition of power *does*, rather than using a label that is associated with the tradition from which it is thought to come. In initially developing these ideas, we used *The Aquarian Conspiracy: Personal and Social Transformation in the 1980s* (by Marilyn Ferguson, Los Angeles: J.P. Tarcher, Inc., 1980) as a point of reference. Ferguson did not identify the prevailing power model as "patriarchal," but she did contrast the prevailing model with transforming power modes emerging in the later part of the 20th century. We borrowed a few of her names for various forms of power, but where we did so we conceptualized them from our own feminist frame of reference.

When we were preparing the 3rd edition of this book, Nancy Greenleaf provided the insights and suggestions that led to our inclusion of the patriarchal power of Accumulation, and the Feminist Alternative Power of Distribution. In a letter dated February 7, 1989, after reviewing a near-final draft of the manuscript, Nancy wrote: "I found myself wanting to add to your power model . . . something that addresses the power of the "free market"; a godlike 'invisible hand' that sorts the worthy from the undeserving and assumes "self-interest" as a primary motivational force. This notion of power is inextricably combined with patriarchal notions, but it specifically addresses material (economic) well being. The feminist alternative is the power that accrues through material sharing—of food, of land or space, and the de-emphasis on privatization of property. The feminist alternative would mean a commitment to bear witness to and expose material inequality."

Charlene and I named and described the feminist alternatives, now called the PEACE powers, from a wide range of feminist theory, as well as our own experiences working in feminist groups. It is impossible to list here all the sources that influenced the creation of this model; however in addition to the sources cited in Chapter One, the following sources were particularly important to us:

Louise Bernikow, *Among Women*. New York: Harmony Books, 1980.

Charlotte Bunch, *Passionate Politics: Feminist Theory in Action*. New York: St. Martin's Press, 1987.

Mary Daly, Gyn/Ecology: *The Metaethics of Radical Feminism,* 1978; *Pure Lust: Elemental Feminist Philosophy,* 1984; and *Websters' First New*

Intergalactic Wickedary of the English Language (in cahoots with Jane Caputi), 1987. All titles published by Beacon Press, Boston, MA.

Andrea Dworkin, *Right-Wing Women*. New York: Perigee Books, 1983.

Riane Eisler, *The Chalice and The Blade*. San Francisco: Harper and Row, 1987.

Susan Griffin, *Woman and Nature: The Roaring Inside Her*. New York: Harper Colophon Books, 1978.

Sarah Lucia Hoagland, *Lesbian Ethics: Toward New Value*. Palo Alto, Institute of Lesbian Studies, 1988.

bell hooks, *Feminist Theory: From Margin to Center*. Boston: South End Press, 1984.

Pam McAllister, (ed): *Reweaving the Web of Life: Feminism and Non-violence*. Philadelphia: New Society Publisher, 1982.

Kate Millett, *Sexual Politics*. New York: Avon Books, 1969.

Cherrie Moraga, and Gloria Anzaldua (eds): *This Bridge Called My Back:* Writings by Radical Women of Color. Watertown, MA: Persephone Press, 1981.

Robin Morgan, (ed): *Sisterhood is Powerful: An Anthology of Writings From the Women's Liberation Movement*. New York: Vintage Books, 1970.

Nel Noddings, *Women and Evil*. Berkeley: University of California Press, 1989.

Adrienne Rich, *On Lies, Secrets and Silence: Selected Prose 1966–1978*. New York: W.W. Norton, 1979.

Chapter Four

1. Margo Adair, *Working Inside Out: Tools for Change*. Berkeley: Wingbow Press, 1984, p. 284. This is a powerful, healing book that provides useful tools for bringing together the personal, spiritual and political aspects of our lives, individually and collectively.

2. Kathleen MacPherson first identified four components around which the Menopause Collective formed their Principles of Unity. Her experience is related in her doctoral dissertation, completed in 1986 at

Brandeis University, titled "Feminist Praxis in the Making: The Menopause Collective." These *Peace and Power* components draw on Kathleen's ideas, as well as the ideas and experience of the Friendship Collective, which worked extensively to develop Principles of Unity.

3. For more information about the early work of the Friendship Collective, see: "Just Between Friends: AJN Friendship Survey," November 1987, pp. 1456–58, and "Friends on Friendship," *American Journal of Nursing,* August 1988, pp. 1094–96. The members of the Friendship Collective are named in this book's "Acknowledgments."

Chapter Five

1. Groups that range from 6 to 50 in number have used *Peace and Power* processes. In groups smaller than 6, it is easy to "skip" the process and slide into a more social interaction. In groups as large as 50, the process has provided for everyone a sense of being included and fully participating.

2. In *Pure Lust,* Boston: Beacon Press, 1984, Mary Daly states: "First of all, Gnomic Nags should note that Real Presence implies being presentient—'feeling or perceiving beforehand.' . . . When women are Present to our Selves, . . . to be presentient is to be animated with hope. This presentient Presence is Positively Powerful, for it implies our capacity to presentiate, that is 'to make or render present in place or time; to cause to be perceived or realized as present' (O.E.D.). Real Presence of the Self, then, which is participation in Powers of Be-ing, implies powers to Realize as present our past and future Selves" (pp. 147–148).

3. Susan Cady, Marian Ronan and Hal Taussig, *SOPHIA: The Future of Feminist Spirituality,* San Francisco: Harper and Row, 1986. Jane Caputi also elaborates on the ancient meanings of Sophia in *Gossips, Gorgons & Crones,* Santa Fe, NM: Bear and Company Publishing, 1993.

Chapter Six

1. We appreciate Anne Montes from Buffalo, New York, for suggesting the idea and for sharing her insights for Random Ravings.

Chapter Seven

1. The Center for Conflict Resolution book entitled *Building United Judgement: A Handbook for Consensus Decision Making* (1981), provides an excellent and in-depth discussion of the processes, possibilities, and challenges of using consensus decision making. These questions are informed by many of their suggestions and insights. Their address is 731 State Street, Madison, WI 53703.

Chapter Eight

1. When Charlene and I were in the Emma Collective, the Collective used this guideline for a four-part criticism as published by Issues in Radical Therapy in 1976 in a small handbook by Gracie Lyons, *Constructive Criticism: A Handbook*. For years, Gracie's book was out of print and we were not able to locate it. In 1988, it was re-published in a revised edition by Wingbow Press. It is distributed by Bookpeople, 2929 Fifth St., Berkeley, CA 94710. The revision remains one of the best resources for developing this important skill. The *Peace and Power* approach to critical reflection draws on Gracie's practical guidelines. In addition, many of her suggestions are integrated into our approaches for conflict transformation.

2. Margo Adair, *Working Inside Out: Tools for Change*. Berkeley: Wingbow Press, 1984. For specific information on how to use affirmations in your personal life to create change, see Chapter Three, "Creating a Language to Speak to Your Deeper Self."

3. From Margo Adair's book in the previous note, p. 46.

4. Notice that these questions are drawn directly from PEACE, the intent with which you enter the process. See Chapter 1.

5. In an article titled "With Gossip Aforethought" in the first issue of *Gossip: A Journal of Lesbian Feminist Ethics,* Anna Livia explains the importance of naming the agent and the source of information to build trust, especially when verbal stories we tell one another are our primary, if not only, way to find out what we need to know to work together. "It is reasonable to ask where a particular piece of gossip comes from. If a lesbian refuses to say, it is ostensibly to protect herself and her source. Why does she need protection, and from whom, if she repeats truthfully what she believes to be the truth? . . . If you won't say how you know [about a person or situation], are we to think you made it up yourself?"

(p. 62). *Gossip* is published by Onlywomen Press, Ltd., 38 Mount Pleasant, London WC1X OAP.

6.   Gracie Lyon's book (see first note, p. 121) has excellent lists of feeling words to help sort out words that carry blame from words that only own a feeling.

7.   Elizabeth Berrey from Cleveland, Ohio, created and owned this as her affirmation in the Friendship Collective. It is a statement that reflects what she has meant to many friends and colleagues, over and over again, in the work and play of living.

Chapter Nine

1.   It is sometimes instructional to browse the dictionary for definitions of words, to clarify what the words have come to mean in popular usage, but additionally for the convoluted and interrelated shades of meanings attached to them. For instance, in *Webster's New Collegiate Dictionary* definitions of conflict speak of "competitive or opposing action of incompatibles"; "hostile encounter." *The American Heritage Dictionary* starts right out with "a prolonged battle, a controversy; disagreement; opposition" and goes on to clarify the differences between conflict and contest (apparently the degree of force involved makes a difference!) Going on to look up "hostile" we encounter words like "enemy, enmity, not hospitable, unfriendly." Little wonder that it is difficult to embrace conflict as a potentially growth producing experience!

2.   Suzette Haden Elgin has written a number of books dealing with the *Gentle Art of Verbal Self-Defense,* ranging from *More on . . .* to *The Last Word On . . . Staying Well With . . .* and *Success With . . .* All of them are excellent and full of information about her approach to modes of communication and ways to break negative communication loops. The techniques she recommends and the responses outlined are manageable and relatively easy to learn. You can practice her suggestions every day and begin to see far-reaching changes—many of which will improve your personal health and well-being.

3.   Suzette Haden Elgin, *Staying Well with the Gentle Art of Verbal Self-Defense,* (Englewood, NJ: Prentice Hall, 1990).

4.   In *Staying Well . . . ,* p. 7.

5.   In *Staying Well . . .,* p. 23.

6. Notice that in a critical reflection you also state what you want to happen next. Also, the "Because . . ." part of a critical reflection focuses on the group's purposes and principles of unity, rather than only an individual reason for addressing the issue.

7. See pages 29–37 in *Staying Well*.

8. In Dale Spender's *Man-Made Language* (Second Edition, Pandora Press, 1985) she includes a poem at the beginning that starts with the line:

"What men dub tattle gossip women's talk
is really revolutionary activity. . ."

She goes on to note ". . . we will have to invest the language with our own authentic meanings, and repudiate many of those which are currently accepted as accurate . . ." (p. 5).

9. Mary Daly in Cahoots with Jane Caputi, *Websters' First Intergalactic Wickedary of the English Language* (Boston: Beacon Press, 1987). This book has a lively discussion of "Gossip" both as noun and as verb in Word-Web Two. Jane Caputi, in *Gossips, Gorgons & Crones: The Fates of the Earth* (Santa Fe: Bear & Company Publishing, 1993), expands on historical women's meanings of gossip, and shows how gossip is needed now to overcome the toxic effects of the nuclear age.

10. Peggy L. Chinn, "Gossip: A Transformative Art for Nursing Education," in the *Journal of Nursing Education* 29:7 (September 1990), pp. 318–321.

11. A book that I have found particularly helpful is *The Dance Of Anger* by Harriet Goldhor Lerner. It is a book written especially for women who have learned to fear anger. The approaches to dealing with anger are safe, constructive and, most of all, achievable. She provides useful and practical guidelines for changing interactions so that everyone involved benefits.

12. These examples grew out of my experience with an extremely divisive work group. With Charlene's wonderful sense of humor and assistance, I began to place myself in others' shoes to try to appreciate in neutral terms what was happening and in order to understand their perspectives in a positive light. We then imagined what things might be like in a group that valued diversity. I shared this with the group at the beginning of a retreat, and we did experience a more positive group interaction for that day.

Chapter Eleven

1.   Kathleen Weiler, *Women Teaching for Change: Gender, Class & Power*. (Massachusetts: Bergin & Garvey Publishers, Inc., 1988), p. 152.

2.   Professor Judy Lumby in Sydney, Australia, relates her experience using *Peace and Power* in teaching college nursing students:

> "We mainly used the checking in and closing processes but all were aware of why these were important. Students evaluated the course very highly. They spoke about how at first they felt that the setting and the process was foreign, but they soon felt comfortable (after about three weeks) and felt able to share in a way which had not been possible before. They certainly shared some wonderful stories of care from the past and present and we reflected and critiqued each other's stories to try to understand the 'why' behind our actions and how it might have been different. We found some similarities in our fears, concerns and beliefs about nursing. Students who I now meet in the ward speak about the course and say that the process was amazing for them."

About the Author

Peggy L. Chinn, PhD, RN, FAAN, is professor of nursing at the University of Colorado Health Sciences Center School of Nursing in Denver, Colorado. She is the founding editor of *Advances in Nursing Science*. Her nursing practice has been in the areas of Child Health and Women's Health. She has published books and journal articles on child health, nursing theory development, nursing education, and feminism. She lives with three canine companions—Sophia, Cozie and Sara, and nurtures things that grow year-round. She is trained in mediation and conflict resolution, and is available for consultation related to all *Peace and Power* processes.